TAX Cafe™

Taxcafe.co.uk Property Guides

How to Profit from Off-Plan Property

By Alyssa and David Savage

Important Legal Notices:

TAXCafe™
"How to Profit from Off-Plan Property"

Published by:
Taxcafe UK Limited
214 High St
Kirkcaldy KY1 1JT
Tel: (0044) 01592 560081
Email: team@taxcafe.co.uk

First Edition, November 2005

ISBN 1 904608 30 2

Disclaimer
Before reading or relying on the content of this book please read carefully the disclaimer on the last page which applies. If you have any queries then please contact the publisher at team@taxcafe.co.uk.

About The Authors

Alyssa and David Savage are the co-founders of Hattan and Grand, a property investment company which sources off-plan and new-build properties for private investors.

Over the last four years they have been involved in the purchase of over £100 million of off-plan and new-build investment property.

Thanks

We would like to thank David Carmichael of Savills Private Finance for his assistance throughout the book. Thanks also go to Chris Tulips of Strefford Tulips for his continuous and welcome advice. A large thank you to Mark Harris of Savills Private Finance for reading through the draft manuscript. Thank you to Steven Aitkin - for just being Steven! Thanks to G.Q.N. for saying if we wanted to write a book, we really should – so we did! We cannot possibly forget Nick Braun of Taxcafe, who not only supported our ideas all the way through - but had the fun job of editing.

Our biggest thank you is to the many investors who have contacted us in the past and, with their queries, helped us to realise that the information and knowledge we held really did need to be made easily accessible to others interested in investing in property.

For my mother, Faye, who has always supported me and my ideas, and has always said that I should write a book - Alyssa

Contents

Foreword

Let me take you to a big city in the north of Britain some time in early 2003.

An impressive advertising campaign has led up to the release of a very large and daring residential property development, promising to breathe new life into a run-down and previously overlooked area of the city.

A queue of potential buyers stretches away from the sales office on the building site – bedrolls and flasks of soup reveal that some people have been there for some time. A man out walking his dog wonders what all the fuss is about and, caught up in the excitement, joins the queue himself. At 9am on the dot the site office opens for business.

The next day local newspapers scream out headlines such as "£48 Million of Property Sold within 24 Hours!" And all this without a single brick having been laid.

Now let's fast forward 18 months. With just over half of the development complete it lies almost empty, a ghetto of 'To Let' and 'For Sale' signs.

Around the country people are facing financial ruin. Some have lost their family homes and some are being taken to court by the developer. Prices and demand in the area have slumped and people in the property industry are starting to ask questions. The man with the dog? Who knows what happened to him.

So why did the above property investment tale have such an unhappy ending for so many people?

In early 2003 the property market was booming. Interest rates were at an historic 37-year low and everybody was trying to jump on the bandwagon.

The people investing in this development were somewhat wet behind the ears. They reserved their apartments without knowing about mortgage shortfalls (discussed later in the book) and, indeed, without realising that one day they would need to have a mortgage.

Almost every investor was planning to reserve an apartment for £500 and then sell the contract on before the completion date, amassing a tidy profit in the process.

After all, the property market was booming, wasn't it? Demand outstripped supply, didn't it?

I know this development intimately for a number of reasons. Several months *before* the queues started forming, my company was given the opportunity to sell units in the development at a 15% discount.

After doing some research, we found that the rental income required to cover a buy-to-let mortgage on the cheapest unit stood at around £1,000 per month. The numbers just didn't stack up. There was no way properties in this area could earn rents of that magnitude.

A more realistic figure would have been between £550 and £800. But with the development full of investors all competing to find tenants, the market rent could easily have fallen below these levels.

The apartments were located in a regeneration area and there were big plans on the drawing board but these were far off in the future. There was no infrastructure to support such a large development and there wouldn't be for several years to come.

And to top it all these 'luxury apartments' were also sited just across from a large sewage plant – a perfect view from your luxury balcony on a hot summer day!

After the investors had reserved their properties and the newspaper headlines had died down, our phones started to ring with people desperately trying to offload their apartments.

One man had reserved five apartments at close to £300,000 each. When I explained to him that he could be facing a mortgage shortfall of close to £80,000 on *each* of his apartments, he was incredulous.

He thought his costs began and ended with his reservation fee of £500 per apartment.

When I had a chance to compare the prices the investors were paying with the prices I had been offered many months earlier, I quickly realised that the new price tags were even *higher* than the ones we had rejected.

If the investment didn't make sense at the previously discounted prices, these new numbers certainly wouldn't stack up!

Almost all of the investors in this development had the sole intention of reserving an apartment for £500 and then re-selling the contracts in a 'back-to-back' transaction, making a quick profit of £50,000 or more – at least that was their intention.

Unfortunately, things don't always work out this way, as many found out to their cost.

What happens if you can't find a buyer or a potential buyer falls through at the last moment? These are just some of the questions the investors didn't even dare to think about.

I had the opportunity of seeing a copy of the contracts the investors had signed. They expressly forbade the advertising or marketing of the properties until the full development was complete... some five years later.

In addition, displaying 'For Sale' signs on the property would not be tolerated. These were just some of the restrictions that would severely hamper any attempt to realise a profit from the property. (The developer had obviously either relented on this clause or buyers, desperate to sell, were simply ignoring it.)

Unfortunately I couldn't help all the investors who came to me for help, as some were already legally obliged to purchase their properties. All I could do was show them what sort of shortfall they might have to make up out of their own pockets and the problems they might experience when it came time to complete. Of all the people I spoke to, not one had consulted a mortgage broker prior to reserving the property.

By coincidence I had the opportunity of meeting with the managing director of the company building this development many months later about a completely separate matter. During the course of our discussions I thought 'what the heck!' and tried to find out just how much he understood about buy-to-let mortgages.

We started talking about the development and what a great response his company had had for the launch. I let the developer know that quite a few people had contacted us at our offices and that I found it incredible that none of them really seemed to understand how buy-to-let mortgages worked.

And then he dropped the bombshell: "How do buy-to-let-mortgages work?"

So I told him. I explained what a mortgage shortfall was. And I showed him how big a shortfall a buy-to-let investor could expect to pay on even his cheapest apartment. I could see it all starting to sink in. But, alas, it was too late. His buyers had already reserved and exchanged contracts. If any one of them was unable to complete, he would have a tough job on his hands recovering the outstanding money.

You see, until recently developers have not had to deal with investors *en masse*. Of course there have always been investors involved in their developments, but not to the extent that they are today.

In fact, we are now seeing what I call the 'reverse iceberg effect'. Five to ten years ago it was mostly prospective home owners who were purchasing their properties from developers. Now, in many instances, the majority are investors.

Up until recently, developers never really needed to understand buy-to-let mortgages and the importance of rental yields and shortfalls – these matters simply didn't affect them. The investors involved in their earlier developments were generally savvy, educated buyers, often with serious money – not the novices of today who want to make a quick buck and don't fully understand the purchasing process or the financial implications.

So, how does this story end? Well, there are a number of endings that have come to my attention.

Firstly, the initial phase of the development was finally built and contract completion got under way.

I received a phone call from one of the people who initially contacted me some 18 months earlier. He was practically begging for help. He went ahead and exchanged contracts rather than walk away from his £500 reservation fee, which had been an option earlier on.

Come completion day his mortgage shortfall was £60,000. He simply did not have this amount of cash at hand. As a result he was not able to complete on the date set by the developer, who started charging him 8% interest, compounded daily, on the outstanding debt.

Nobody wanted to buy his apartment because there were so many other people in exactly the same situation, so much so that potential buyers had become wary of the development.

The last time I heard from this man he had had to sell his home, uproot his children from their school and friends and move into the apartment. He was also facing a daily commute of up to three hours each way to get to work.

If he had simply done his research and understood the potential risks of purchasing off plan he may not have found himself in this position in the first place.

As it happens he was informed about all the dangers when he discussed his purchase with me and could have simply walked away from his £500 non-refundable reservation fee.

Another sorry tale brought to my attention was one of property 'pass the parcel' – a contract to buy an apartment that was 'sold on' five times before the property was completed.

Each time the contract was 'sold on' the property became a little more expensive, providing the seller each time with a modest profit. But if the property was unworkable from a buy-to-let perspective at the original price, how could it be workable at these higher prices? That's right, it wasn't.

So, if the fifth buyer was unable to complete the purchase, who was liable to pay the developer? Well it was actually the *initial buyer* who remained liable. The initial buyer thought that he had sold the property to someone else and had nothing to worry about. As it turned out, he was still legally obliged to buy it.

He could either complete the purchase or be charged interest and eventually be sued by the developer. He would then most likely have to sue the person he sold the contract to, who in turn would have to sue the next buyer and so on.

The last I heard through the grapevine was that the lender pulled the plug on the final phase of the development. The chances are that the developer was not able to pay back the initial loan for the first phase due to the number of people unable to complete. What a mess!

*

The moral of this story?

Obviously, it's crucial to understand all the risks involved in purchasing off-plan property. Knowing how buy-to-let mortgages work, what shortfalls are and how you calculate them, how back-to-back transactions work, and why you need an independent survey are all critical to your success as an off-plan investor.

Being an *educated investor* is what it's all about. Understanding the difference between a potentially good deal and a disaster in the making is crucial.

And that's why I decided to write this book. Buying off-plan property is still a great way to make a profit, whether it be short-term speculation or long-term investment. However, you have to be an educated investor to reap the rewards.

I would also encourage investors to take a second look at what they are buying. In many city centres there has been, and continues to be, a glut of new-build properties for sale. Why? Because, in many cases, these new developments are entirely investor-driven.

Investor activity has changed the property landscape in many parts of the country. In many cases, investors have bought overpriced apartments and then tried to increase those prices further in order to make a profit.

Those renting out their properties often have to charge a fairly hefty rent just to service their mortgages. These rents are often higher than the local market can bear. This can result in many apartments within a development lying empty, or rented out for a sum far below what is required to meet the mortgage payments.

Go to any property investment show these days and you will be swamped by salesmen in shiny suits selling off-plan property. You never see them offering £60,000 tenement flats in Dundee and such like. Instead they'll be trying to offload units in some or other new apartment block.

Invariably you'll be offered a 'discount' or 'guaranteed rental income' and almost invariably you should run a mile. Why? Because these carrots are often artificially created simply by raising the list price of the property.

Even if they are genuine you should always think twice about buying property where there are lots of other investors trying to do the same thing. How are you going to rent out or sell your fancy new apartment if there are dozens of other investors with equally fancy apartments trying to do the same thing?

I call these investor ghettos.

The purpose of this book is to teach you everything I know about buying off-plan property: How to make solid long-term investments... and the occasional quick profit!

You'll also learn from the many disasters I've witnessed over the years and find out how to avoid the numerous traps and pitfalls.

It is my belief that investors should arm themselves with as much information as possible before parting with a single penny.

I do hope that you find this book useful and easy to read.

Alyssa Savage
November, 2005

Chapter 1

How (Not) to Become a Property Millionaire!

I am sure that many of you reading this book have seen adverts saying something along the lines of: 'Become a Property Millionaire in Less than a Year'.

You may also have met people who claim to be property millionaires and you think, "Wow, if only that were me. I've got to get on the property bandwagon to financial freedom."

The funny thing is that most of these people really aren't millionaires at all.

Over the years, I have met many people who make this sort of claim. Here's how our conversation usually goes:

Investor: "I own over £1 million in property, and I did that in less than a year!"

Me: "Wow, good for you. So are you telling me that you have no mortgages on these properties?"

Investor: "No. I am planning on selling them on from plan!"

Me: "Ok, so are you telling me that they aren't built yet?"

Investor: "Yes. I just reserved four apartments valued at £250,000 each, but I bought them at £200,000 each!"

Me: "So you are saying that you haven't completed on them? You haven't sold them, and they are still being built?"

Investor: "Yes. They only cost me £2,000 in reservation fees."

Me: "So tell me, are you going to have buy-to-let mortgages in place?"

Investor: "No. I don't need any."

Me: "Ok, so you are saying that you are paying cash for each unit?"

Investor: "You have to be joking! I don't have that kind of money!"

Me: "Are you telling me that you didn't get in touch with a lender or mortgage broker before you reserved?"

Investor: "No. Because I'm selling them before I complete."

Me: "Have you had these properties surveyed?"

Investor: "Yes. The property investment company I am using told me that an estate agent valued them at £250,000, and I am getting them for £200,000! So I am going to make at least £50,000 per unit!"

Me: "I take it that you haven't even exchanged contracts yet?"

Investor: "What is that?"

Me: "Is the developer not asking for a deposit when you exchange contracts."

Investor: "Yes. I'll use some of the profit from selling the properties for this."

Me: "Are you aware that exchange of contracts will happen approximately 28 days after you reserve? Are you aware that you will have to come up with the deposit the developer is asking for – usually 10% - plus other fees at this stage?"

Investor: "Oh, I didn't know that."

Me: "Do you have a 10% deposit plus funds for other fees available, *per property*?"

Investor: "No."

Me: "From what you are saying it sounds like you can't even afford to exchange contracts! You are looking at around £80,000 in deposits alone in less than a month."

Investor: "I can always re-mortgage my home for these funds."

Me: "Well good luck. If you haven't started that process already you will be very lucky to release funds within a month. My other concern is that you are not applying for a mortgage. What happens if you are unable to sell the properties that quickly?"

Investor: "Well, I'll just keep them until I find a buyer."

Me: "I don't think you quite understand. The developer will set a completion date for your property, at which point you must provide them with the remaining funds. If you don't have a mortgage in place the developer will charge you interest compounded daily. Or they may sue you. Remember, the property is not legally yours until you complete."

Investor: "I didn't realise that."

Me: "My other concern is rental values."

Investor: "Yes, but I'm not going to rent them out, as I keep telling you – I am going to sell them, so it doesn't really matter what the rent is."

Me: "Well, were you not told that most buy-to-let mortgages are based on rental valuations? Lenders want evidence that the potential rental income will easily cover your mortgage payments."

Investor: "I know a friendly letting agent who will say that the rental income is high enough."

Me: "It doesn't quite work like that! It will be the lender's surveyor who will decide what the rental value is – not your friendly letting agent."

Investor: "Oh."

Me: "This is a very big issue. Do you have any idea what kind of rents these apartments will generate?"

Investor: "Around £850 per month."

Me: "Ok, well let me just work that out for you, using my mortgage calculator. Based on the information you have given me, and using an interest rate of 5.69%, a lender will only loan you £143,409 per apartment. This means that you will have to pay almost £60,000 *for each apartment!* Tell me, do you have £240,000 cash available? And oh, I almost forgot! You also have to pay stamp duty on each unit."

Investor: "But as I mentioned, I am planning on selling my units before I complete."

Me: "How many units are in the whole development?"

Investor: "Around 250."

Me: "And how many units were sold to investors?"

Investor: "All of them."

Me: "Do you really expect to sell them before the completion date, along with all the other investors trying to do the same thing? If it were me, I'd rather take a £2,000 loss rather than have to fork out £250,000!

"Although this deal may sound good with its discount, it simply doesn't stack up!"

Summary

Several important lessons can be learned from this discussion:

- The investor in this example had not completed the purchase of the properties and therefore didn't own them. So stating that he is a property millionaire is very far from the truth!
- He was also under the misconception that after paying a reservation fee of £500 per unit, the properties were his and his profit would automatically be £50,000 per unit (because he bought them at a 'discount').
- The investor's downfall was not understanding how buy-to-let mortgages work and why rental valuations are so important.
- He bought property that hadn't even been valued by an independent RICS surveyor – so who knows whether or not the true value of the properties was £250,000.

Amazingly the investor in the above example had already attended an expensive course about investing in property and yet still didn't understand the basics.

It is this lack of knowledge and incredible desire on the part of so many to get into property investment that has created cracks in the property market, specifically in the area of new-build property.

The Government has already started closing down the numerous get-rich-quick property schemes but this could cause a dangerous wobble in the market for newly built flats, many of which are bought en masse by property clubs and syndicates. In fact, in May 2005 The

Financial Times ran an article stating that prices of new flats had fallen by more than 17% over the preceding 12 months.

How to Become a Property Millionaire... Slowly

All this doesn't mean that buying property from plan isn't a good idea! Far from it. Here are some examples of investors who did get it right and made handsome profits.

As you go through these examples, it is important to note that the discount offered was almost irrelevant to the success or failure of the investment.

A discount should only form part of your decision to buy a property – it should never be the sole reason for your purchase.

Case Study # 1

In December 2002, a two-bedroom unit was purchased for £85,000 by one of our clients who we will call Jane. There was a genuine 15% discount, confirmed by a RICS (Royal Institution of Chartered Surveyors) surveyor.

We were able to negotiate this discount because the developer was fast approaching its financial year end. The company had 12 remaining units that it needed to sell quickly to meet its targets.

Therefore, we agreed to offer these units to our clients and meet the developer's strict deadline. The unit was completed in July 2003 and subsequently sold to someone else for £112,000.

Fortunately Jane had a mortgage in place because the ultimate buyer had a few problems getting his funds through in time for completion. In fact, it was two weeks after the completion date that the new buyer was in a position to complete.

In the end Jane made a gross profit of £27,000 in seven months!

Let's look take a closer look at the deal:

- Original market value: £100,000
- Price paid: £85,000
- Resale price: £112,000
- Investment company fee: £2,350
- Solicitor's fees: £1,000
- Mortgage broker's fee: £850
- Surveyor's fee: £175
- Lender's arrangement fee: £199
- Stamp duty: Stamp duty exempt area
- Estate agent's fee, including advertising: £1,370

Therefore, in just seven months, Jane had a net profit of £21,056, which she used to continue building her property portfolio.

Case Study # 2

In this example the property had already been built. There were just a few units left and the developer wanted to sell them quickly.

The list price was £90,000 but the developer was offering them for £85,000.

Although this wasn't a large discount it was a genuine discount giving equity of £5,000 from day one.

More importantly, the development was in an area starting to experience steady capital growth.

The best buy-to-let mortgage available to this investor was at an interest rate of 5.85% and required 125% rental cover. The potential rental income was verified at £450 per month.

After paying the 15% deposit the investor required a mortgage of £72,250. The maximum buy-to-let mortgage he could expect to raise was £73,846, so the deal stacked up.

Let's look at the costs:

- Reservation fee: £500
- Deposit: £8,500
- Property investment company fee: £2,115
- Solicitor's fees: £1,000
- Stamp duty: Property was in an exempt area
- Mortgage broker's fee: £850
- Lender's arrangement fee: £299
- Remaining deposit required by lender: £4,250
- Survey Fee: £175

The total cost to the buyer was £17,689 plus a further £3,500 to furnish and decorate the property, bringing the total costs to £21,189.

Sounds expensive, doesn't it? But remember that the property was valued at £90,000 giving the purchaser £5,000 immediate equity.

The property rented out immediately for £500 per month, easily covering his monthly mortgage payment of £352.

On top of this, the property was in an area experiencing good capital growth and was recently revalued at £100,000.

As you can see, the £5,000 discount was not the important factor. The area itself, although not considered particularly 'desirable' proved to be an excellent investment choice as the combination of affordable prices and strong rental demand resulted in steady capital growth.

Case Study # 3

Here's an example of a property deal that looked great in the beginning but eventually turned a bit sour. I personally invested in a unit in this prime city centre development in an area that was starting to achieve excellent growth due to regeneration.

The details were as follows:

- The build programme was two years
- The list price was £160,000, supported by a RICS survey
- My purchase price was £143,000
- The expected rental from the property was £750
- Reservation fee: £1,000
- Missives fee: £2,000
- Solicitor's fees: £1,000
- Mortgage broker's fee: £715
- Lender's arrangement fee: £299
- Survey fee: £175
- Stamp duty: £1,430
- Estate agent's fees: £1,500

At the time of purchase, everything was looking good. The rental was high enough to easily cover the mortgage and keep the lender happy and, because I was buying at a discount, I didn't have to pay a deposit thanks to an LTV mortgage package that was available at the time.

When the completion date arrived things weren't looking quite so rosy:

- The lender had withdrawn the buy-to-let mortgage package I wanted due to abuse from borrowers. As a result I now had to stump up a 15% deposit.

- Interest rates had risen four times since I reserved the property. As a result the rent was insufficient to provide the lender with adequate rental cover. This meant I would personally have to stump up what they didn't!

- There was now a glut of similar properties in the area with numerous 'To Let' and 'For Sale' signs everywhere – in many cases the prices were too high for the average buyer.

- As I had already concluded missives on the unit I was legally bound to complete.

I ended up having to fund a 20% deposit in order to provide the cover required by the lender.

I completed and ended up paying the mortgage for three months before selling the property. To ensure a quick sale I had to offer to pay the buyer's stamp duty and pay for flooring.

My gross profit on this deal ended up being just £358!

Could I have done anything differently? I don't think I could have. I saw an opportunity and, at the time, it worked. That's property investment!

The area was well researched and when I reserved the property, prices were growing strongly and this was expected to continue for several years. I had the unit valued by a RICS surveyor and a letting agent – both concluding that the deal did 'stack up'.

Ultimately, I could not control the rise in interest rates or the amount of other investors wanting to get into this particular area.

This experience is a perfect example of why I'm no longer interested in glitzy new developments in major city centres which cost upwards of £150,000.

Instead, I am looking at properties under the £125,000 mark (preferably under £100,000) in outlying areas where rental yields are higher and the deal stacks easier.

I also try and avoid developments in which a lot of the buyers are fellow property investors. Many of these become 'investor ghettos'.

Instead, I look for sites that have just a handful of units left which the developer wants to sell quickly. This way I can more easily find out if the other owners are 'buy to live' homeowners rather than buy-to-let investors.

Buying one of the last remaining units in a development also allows me to accurately assess how much deposit the lender will require as I will be getting a mortgage quickly instead of in, say, two years' time when the property has been built and interest rates and rental values may have changed.

Case Study # 4

Here's an example of a property that I purchased and sold in a 'back-to-back' transaction.

Purchase price: £92,000
Discount: None
Reservation fee: £250
Missives fee: £250
Legal fees: £750
Estate agent fees: £1,250
Mortgage broker fees: £460
Lender's arrangement fee: £299
Survey fee: £175
Build programme: 18 months

I purchased this property without getting a discount off the list price. However, I did secure a special pre-release price which was offered to attract initial buyers into a big development. Provided demand for property continued to rise I stood to make a good profit.

Several weeks prior to completion I put the property on the market through a national estate agent for £115,000. So too did many other investors.

I wanted to sell this unit as quickly as possible so that I wouldn't have to complete and stump up a 15% mortgage deposit. So I decided to drop my price to £110,000 in order to undercut the other investors and ensure a quick sale.

Within a week I had a buyer. Contracts were signed and ultimately a back-to-back transaction occurred. To be on the safe side I also had a mortgage offer in place in case the new buyer pulled out for some reason – I was fully aware that I was still 100% liable for the debt on the property and needed to complete should I not have a buyer in place.

Therefore, I incurred the cost of a survey, the lender's arrangement fees and a mortgage broker's fee. Because I purchased at a reasonable price I was also able to sell at a reasonable price and still make a good profit.

Chapter 2

Why Invest in Off-plan Property?

Individuals and institutions have been investing in property for hundreds of years. However, up until fairly recently, property investment has been the preserve of the wealthy and those who weren't well off rented from those who were.

Changes to legislation in recent years and easy access to buy-to-let mortgages have resulted in people from all walks of life becoming involved in property in one way or another – whether it be buying a dream holiday home in Spain or refurbishing an end-terrace house to make a quick profit.

Off-plan property investment, in particular, has taken the nation by storm in the last five years.

I have been involved in off-plan property purchases of over £100 million to date – note that's £100 million of property that my company *did* agree to offer to clients. At least four times this figure was discarded, simply because it did not meet our criteria.

To be a successful off-plan property investor you have to be extremely fussy.

Why Invest in Property That Hasn't Been Built Yet?

Most people are familiar with the 'normal' way of buying a property – the one where the property actually exists and can be viewed by walking around it.

When purchasing property off-plan all this goes out the window because in many cases the foundations haven't even been laid.

Instead you buy the property from plans provided by the developer along with a price list and specifications of what will be included. From this information, buyers can select the property that is most suited to their needs and budget.

Actual viewing of the property may not occur until several weeks before completion due to health and safety regulations.

The main reason most people invest in off-plan property, or any property for that matter, is to achieve *capital growth.*

Some off-plan investments are extremely speculative, with investors looking to make a quick profit in the time between reserving and building the property.

For this strategy to work you have to either buy at a genuine discount or buy at a time when property prices are rising strongly.

On developments over a certain size builders will generally stagger the release of properties. You may have seen the signs on building sites saying something like: "Phase 1 Sold Out – Phase 2 Now Released!"

What you may also notice, on closer inspection, is that the same house or apartment that was on sale in Phase 1 is now for sale in Phase 2 at a higher price, typically 10% more.

If there are further phased releases, these too will be available at a higher price than the original first phase.

Setting Phase 1 prices quite low is a technique builders use to kick-start developments.

Phase 1 prices are set at a level that generates a lot of interest and some quick sales. Knowing there is enough demand for the properties, prices of further phases can be increased.

This technique can also benefit the off-plan property investor. For example, let's say you exchange contracts (conclude missives in Scotland) for house type 'A', which costs £100,000 in the first phase of a development and takes approximately six months to build.

At the time of completion, the developer is selling houses in the second phase. House type 'A' in this phase is now selling for £112,500. The investor decides to put his property on the market for £110,000 in direct competition with the developer (provided he is not contractually prevented from doing this).

Not counting the various costs such as mortgage payments and solicitor's fees, the investor will have made a gross profit of £10,000 in just six months.

You can often buy at the lowest possible price by reserving a property *before* the development has been released on to the open market. This is where property investment companies are useful as they are generally in a better position to negotiate a deal with the developer prior to general release.

Smaller developments, which most likely will not be phased, can also produce solid capital growth. In fact, smaller developments, in the right location, where there is not a huge amount of competition from other new-build property may in some cases be a better prospect.

The less competition you have from other investors wishing to rent out or re-sell their properties the better.

To recap, one of the main reasons why investors find off-plan investment so exciting is that you can buy property at a genuine discount and benefit from any rise in the property's value *while it is being built.*

Added to this, mortgage payments and the final deposit plus stamp duty are not due until the property has been built.

This means that, for a smaller initial financial outlay than buying an existing property, the investor can buy at today's prices and benefit from any increase in property values, without having to come up with the full funds required until completion.

In some cases this can be up to two years away, depending on the build time.

Other, less important, but no less valid reasons for taking the off-plan property route are the following:

- **Guarantees.** Most new properties come with a 10-year NHBC Warranty or similar, protecting you against building defects. In addition, the developer is generally responsible for any repairs needed on a new home for two years after purchase.

- **No Need for Renovations or Refurbishment**. Off-plan investors don't face unexpected costs (like the need for a new roof, new windows, or re-wiring!) and no refurbishment costs to bring the property up to an acceptable standard.

- **Quick profits.** In some cases off-plan buyers can 'get in on the ground floor' in areas that have not yet seen substantial increases in property values (such as regeneration areas).

Table 1
Pros and Cons of Off-plan Property

Pros

- Capital growth potential during build.
- Staggered payments so costs are spread out.
- Genuine discounts can provide instant profits.
- Nothing to view except plans - so easy to do from anywhere in the world.
- Potential to sell the property in a 'back-to-back' transaction, providing an immediate exit, without the need for a mortgage or to find tenants.
- Most new-build properties come with extensive warranties.
- Opportunities arise to buy in areas that have not yet experienced extensive capital growth.

Cons

- Interest rates may go up or rental and property values may go down while the property is being built.
- There could be a large number of investors trying to sell or rent out properties in the same development.
- It's sometimes difficult to gauge what the property looks like until you see it in the flesh... by then it may be too late.
- Most home buyers want to view the completed property before they commit. As a result you may have to complete the purchase process before reselling.
- Poor workmanship and vast snagging lists on new-build properties may make it difficult to resell or find tenants for many months.

Chapter 3

Off-plan Property: The Buying Process

NOTE: Before you even consider buying a property it is vital that you consult a mortgage broker or lender to confirm that you are able to raise a buy-to-let mortgage.

Buying off-plan property normally goes through the following stages:

- A suitable development is identified.
- Due diligence is carried out to see if it's a good investment.
- Surveyor instructed to confirm the gross price of the property is in line with comparable property in the area.
- Reservation fees are taken and reservation forms signed by the buyer (generally between £250 and £1,000 and in most cases non-refundable).
- Buyer needs to conclude missives (Scotland) 14 days after reservation or exchange contracts (England and Wales) 28 days after reservation. At this stage a deposit will be required by the developer. The investment company (if used) and solicitor fees and disbursement charges will also be required. The average deposit is usually 10% of the purchase price of the property required by the developer.
- Build starts or continues.
- Mortgage offer needs to be in place a few months earlier than completion is expected, as completion can come earlier than initially anticipated.

- Property receives a habitation order (Scotland) or build control passes the property (England) and buyer is expected to complete within a few days of the property receiving this (seven days in Scotland, 10 days in England).

- Completion occurs - funds are paid to your solicitor to cover outstanding deposit plus stamp duty etc, and the solicitor draws the remaining funds from the lender in order to make up the amount of funds owing (minus the reservation fee and deposit already paid in). The Transfer Deed (the document confirming you as the owner) will be sent to the relevant registry.

- Key handover occurs, once the developer's solicitor receives funds.

In this chapter I'll take a closer look at each of these stages. There are two different ways of buying off-plan investment property these days: either using or not using the services of an investment company. I will therefore examine each stage of the buying process both when an investment company is used and not used.

BUYING WITHOUT A PROPERTY INVESTMENT COMPANY

Before you buy any property you should do exhaustive research. You must know as much as possible about the area where the property is located: What rents are similar properties achieving? How much are similar properties selling for? How long are properties sitting on the market? Are buyers looking for family homes or apartments?

Once you've decided to invest in a particular property the buying process goes through a number of stages:

- Decision in principle from mortgage lender
- Reservation
- Survey

- Mortgage application
- Mortgage offer
- Exchange of contracts
- Snagging
- Completion

Your mortgage offer may come after exchange of contracts depending on the build time and the developer's solicitor's stipulations.

Decision in Principle

Prior to reserving any property, it's vital to know whether you can get a mortgage.

The first step in the mortgage process is called a Decision in Principle, or DiP. Some lenders also call this an Acceptance in Principle, or AiP.

The DiP is a preliminary stage and is essentially a credit history check. In many cases the lender or mortgage broker can take your details over the phone and process your information straight away.

If you go directly through a bank or building society then you may receive your DiP within a few minutes. A mortgage broker may take a few days to identify the lender which is best suited to your requirements.

Although time is sometimes of the essence when you want to reserve a property, it's essential that you do not exchange contracts until you have, at the very least, a DiP or even a full mortgage offer.

It's one thing to lose a couple of hundred pounds in reservation fees if you are unable to proceed with the purchase but quite another to have to unexpectedly pay out thousands of pounds come completion.

Even if you receive a DiP, you can still be turned down for a mortgage, particularly if your financial situation changes between receiving your DiP and applying for your mortgage.

Even if you have a perfect credit history, every time you apply for credit, a new entry is made on your credit history report. The more applications you make within a relatively short period of time, the more this can count against you.

Therefore, if you are shopping around for a good mortgage package, be wary of having too many DiPs carried out by a variety of different lenders. My mortgage broker advised me that you should never have more than one credit check within a space of three months (whether for a credit card, store card or mortgage).

I have first-hand experience of this. Not realising at the time that too many credit searches can count against you, I was shopping around for a good mortgage package and obtained a DiP from three different lenders.

Because my credit file showed that different lenders had performed searches on me within a short space of time, when it came time to actually get a mortgage no lender was prepared to give me a loan of more than 80%. I had in fact been counting on getting one for 95% because this was a personal residential mortgage for my family home.

Imagine my shock when I had been budgeting for a 5% deposit, only to find that I was going to need a further 15%. All I can say is that I learned my lesson!

Lastly, with regard to DiPs, some last for six months but others last for only 30 days, depending on the lender.

Experian/Equifax Reports

I would strongly recommend taking the time to request your credit history reports from these companies. The cost is minimal (approximately £2) and asking for them does not count against your credit history.

To order your report online go to www.experian.co.uk and www.equifax.co.uk.

Many clients have told me that when they received their reports they found inaccurate or completely out of date information (such as County Court judgments that had long been settled but still showed as owing on their reports).

Knowledge is power so it is crucial that you know exactly what lenders are going to see when they do background checks on you.

It's also important to get your credit history report sooner rather than later. In other words, even if you are only thinking about buying a new property some time in the future, get your report now. If there are errors on it, it will take time to rectify the situation.

If your report does contain inaccurate information and you are not having any joy resolving the issue it may be worth getting in touch with a legal firm that has a debt recovery section.

Obviously this will cost money but ultimately it is worth having any incorrect information deleted from your credit report. Being able to obtain finance with minimum fuss is critical if you are a property investor.

Also, if you have recently moved home, make sure that you get on to the electoral role at the new address as soon as possible – it's one of the things lenders look for.

Reserving a Property

All developers require a reservation fee upfront in order to hold a property in your name. Once you've reserved the property, it will not be available to other buyers unless you fail to exchange contracts.

Reservation fees vary but tend to be more expensive if the property is being bought as an investment. Fees for investment property are generally between £500 and £1,000. Fees for personal-use residential property can be as low as £250.

If you do not go ahead and exchange contracts it's quite common for developers to keep your reservation fee. The reservation form should state clearly whether the fee is wholly or partly refundable.

Make sure that you have your solicitor's full mailing address and phone number as this is usually asked for on the form.

Once you reserve a property the next stages in the purchase process can happen quite quickly. Your reservation form will be passed on to the developer's solicitor in order to draw up the contracts. As soon as these are complete, which could be within days, they will be sent to your solicitor.

At the time of reservation you will be given an indication as to when your property is expected to be completed. Obviously the shorter the build programme the easier it is for the developer to pinpoint the completion date.

However, you should never rely too much on these dates as they can change dramatically. I have seen developments completed nine months late and several months earlier than anticipated. Both situations can cause problems if you are not prepared, for example if the development is ahead of schedule and your mortgage offer is not in place.

As soon as you reserve your property it is important to notify your solicitor, providing full details of the property, so that he can verify these facts when he receives the contracts.

Also inform your mortgage broker that you have reserved and when the completion date is expected so that he can work to this date.

From the date that your solicitor receives your contracts you will have approximately 28 days to exchange contracts in England and Wales and approximately 14 days to conclude missives in Scotland.

Because things happen so quickly it's vital to have funds in place to pay the developer's deposit and any other fees before you even reserve a property.

Survey

When you inform your mortgage broker that you have reserved a property ask him to instruct a survey for you. The surveyor should be on your chosen lender's approved panel of RICS surveyors.

The survey should be carried out prior to exchanging contracts in order to confirm that the gross price of the property is in line with the current market value of comparable properties in the area.

If you have been offered a discount, now is also the time to find out whether it is, in fact, genuine! Never give the surveyor the discounted price of your property, always give him the 'gross' price. If the surveyor agrees that the gross price is acceptable, then your discount is most likely genuine.

Even if the developer tells you that you are paying less than the 'list price', this doesn't mean that you are getting a genuine discount. The developer's list prices may be out of line with property prices in the area. If the property is only worth what you have to pay you are not getting a genuine discount.

Many investors have been caught out by believing that whatever the developer's list prices are must be the current local market value. Unfortunately this is not always the case.

It's essential to have a valuation carried out prior to exchanging contracts, because after that it's too late to pull out and you may be legally committed to buying an overpriced property.

If the property is far from being finished, the surveyor will carry out what is called a 'desktop survey' based on the property's plans and comparables (similar properties in the area). You should also request that the surveyor provide you with rental valuations as well.

Exchange of Contracts

Up until you exchange contracts, either you or the developer can back out of the purchase with no legal comeback. If a developer withdraws, the company will need to refund your full reservation fee.

However, if you withdraw, then it is very likely that you will not get your reservation fee back.

When you exchange contracts you are legally obliged to buy the property at the price listed in the contract and comply with all the other terms and conditions.

English and Scottish property law differ in a variety of ways. In England and Wales if you do not complete, the developer can legally pursue you for 10% of the purchase price to cover costs such as advertising and marketing expenses. However, in Scotland the penalty can be much stiffer and the vendor can sue you for not completing.

When the contracts are received from the developer's solicitor it is important that you **read them** to confirm the price and plot number are correct, that you are happy with the terms and then sign and return them with the correct amount of money promptly. I always encourage people to send any legal documents and/or cheques by registered mail to ensure that they arrive safely and on time.

Tighter money laundering regulations mean that you will be required to provide photo identification to both your solicitor and the mortgage broker, and sometimes even the developer, before they are able to proceed with your transaction. Therefore it is important to have a current driver's licence or passport.

Sometimes off-plan deals are extremely time sensitive and it is important to honour the deadline. Remember, up until exchange of contracts takes place the developer can pull the plug on the sale and you could lose out on a potentially lucrative investment opportunity.

With longer term build programmes it is unlikely that you will hear anything further from your solicitor or the developer for many months once you have exchanged contracts. However, I think that every few months it is good practice to check in with the developer to find out if they are on target to meet the completion date.

Mortgage Offer

Mortgage offers generally last for only six months. It is important, therefore, to get your timing right so that you are covered should your property complete early or later than initially expected. Most offers can, however, be extended should the need arise.

You may even need to have a mortgage offer before exchange of contracts, even if completion is up to two years away! Ask your solicitor to check with the developer's solicitor as you may need to get rolling with a mortgage application promptly in order to meet the exchange deadline. Your solicitor may also require your mortgage offer before exchange of contracts.

It is very important that you double check everything on your mortgage application form before signing it. This is particularly important if a mortgage broker has completed part of the form for you.

Dates, names, addresses and facts and figures must all be correct. If your details do not match the information contained in your credit report then your mortgage application may be delayed or even rejected. Once again, this is why it's important to get hold of your Experian or Equifax report before applying.

If a significant amount of time has elapsed since the first survey was carried out, your mortgage broker or lender will instruct another one to ascertain the current value of the property closer to completion.

Snagging

Snagging is the process whereby all the problems with the property are identified and fixed. Most new-build properties suffer from snagging issues.

Snagging should take place before completion. The developer should give you the opportunity to view the property at least a couple of days before legal completion. This will allow you to identify any outstanding problems that need to be fixed.

The developer is then responsible for ensuring that all the issues you identified are addressed. It is important to note that, in many cases, these issues are not always taken care of prior to completion.

Some investors may think that if there are outstanding snagging issues they will not need to complete until these are sorted out. Sadly, this is not the case.

For detailed information about snagging go to Chapter 11.

Completion

When the completion date arrives, your mortgage funds are drawn down and transferred to the developer, solicitors finalise the contracts and the keys are handed over. The property is now yours.

Typically, it is only now that you will be able to enter the property to lay flooring or install window coverings. It is also only now that you will be able to show your property to prospective tenants or buyers.

BUYING THROUGH A PROPERTY INVESTMENT COMPANY

There are three important reasons why you may want to use a property investment company to buy off-plan property:

- They can negotiate deals, such as discounts of 10-15%, or more, that are not available to individual investors who lack the same bulk-buying power.
- They can provide you with detailed research into the investment merits of an off-plan development.
- They can hold your hand through all aspects of the purchasing process.

A good property investment company will subject prospective developments to stringent due diligence before offering them to investors.

I say 'good' because there are many property investment companies out there that are downright terrible! In fact, some are actually boiler room operations that have disappeared overnight with investors' money.

It's important to remember that the UK property investment market is unregulated. Almost anyone can set up a property investment company and offer advice and deals to investors.

It's also important to remember that if you use a property investment company, its services do not come free. You will pay approximately 2% commission on any property you buy.

You should not pay commission simply for being introduced to an investment opportunity. You should also receive detailed research as to the viability of the investment.

Although there may be occasions when you have to make a snap decision to secure a property, you should never let a pushy property investment company pressurise you into buying a property.

And never buy property on the basis of information given over the phone by a salesman. You would never buy your own house this way, so don't buy investment property this way either.

Make sure you have as much information as possible prior to reserving.

Below are details of the off-plan buying process when a property investment company is used.

Due Diligence

When you are contacted about a new property investment opportunity the first thing you should receive is detailed information about the development and the local area, including:

The development

- Details of any discount being offered.
- A RICS survey confirming that list, or gross, prices are in line with current market values. This means the discount is most likely to be genuine.
- At least two letters from local letting agents confirming how much rent the properties are likely to achieve.
- The number of units in the development.
- The number of units being sold to investors – the fewer the better.
- Parking – is it included in the purchase price? If not, will this affect the sale price? Will it affect the rental values? Is parking available at an additional cost and if so, how much?

- The size of the reservation fee. It is recommended that this should not be paid to the property investment company but to the developer's solicitor in order to maintain transparency.
- The amount of deposit required by the developer on exchange of contracts.
- Details of any solicitor who will be acting on your behalf, or can you use your own solicitor?
- The completion date for the development.
- Full details of specifications, including fixtures and fittings, appliances, painting, tiling, flooring (many do not provide flooring), security systems and door entry systems.

Demographics and Area

- Details of the local area and its property market.
- Growth in property prices over the past few years.
- Average rental income for similar properties.
- Proximity to transportation links, schools and hospitals.
- Population, employment and crime statistics.
- Is the development in a regeneration area?
- What is the Local Authority's regeneration strategy?
- Are there other new developments in the area and what level of competition can be expected? What prices are other new-build properties starting at?

In some cases new developments can sell out very quickly. However, it's important not to get caught up in the excitement. One thing I've learned over the years is that no deal is ever a 'once in a lifetime opportunity'. If you miss out there will always be a next time.

However, if the deal is a good one, it is important to act quickly to secure a property in your name but only if you have all the pertinent information.

Reservation

Although you may have to pay your reservation fee quickly to secure a property, a reputable investment company will not submit your cheque until you have a received a Decision in Principle from a lender and a copy of the survey.

This should give you at least a few days to carry out your own due diligence before the company submits your payment.

Much of what happens next is identical to buying the property without the help of a property investment company. The only difference is that the property investment company will work closely with its nominated professionals and the investor to ensure that the whole process is smooth and painless.

Once you are happy with the survey and have received a Decision in Principle from the mortgage lender, the investment company will submit your reservation fee to the developer. The developer will then instruct its solicitor to draw up contracts.

Tip

If you are paying your reservation fee directly to the property investment company make sure you know who the actual vendor is.

I am aware of several property investment companies who actually exchange contracts with the developer themselves and then sell the properties on to their clients.

By doing this they lose all objectivity when marketing the properties to their clients. Furthermore, because the investment company will be making a profit by selling the properties for more than it paid for them, this obviously reduces the profit margins for investors.

Usually the only winner in this scenario is the property investment company.

Lastly, make sure you get a receipt whenever you make any payments.

Exchange of Contracts

This process will be similar to that outlined above.

Mortgage Offer and Completion

Generally, as the development nears physical completion, the developer will either contact you directly or contact the investment company with an expected completion date.

The investment company should then ensure that you are aware of this date so that you can get your mortgage in place.

Snagging

As mentioned earlier, snagging generally takes place before completion. A good investment company will be able to use its bulk-buying power to negotiate a discount for its clients from a professional snagging company.

Your investment company should arrange everything for you. It is important to note that, regardless of snagging issues, you are still required to complete on time. (For more about snagging see Chapter 11.)

Letting

A good property investment company will have contacts with several letting agents in the area where the development is situated. Some may also have negotiated a discount on the letting agent's fees.

Furnishings

If you want to rent out your property you are going to have to furnish it to a high standard. Your investment company should have a number of suitable furnishing companies on its books. Once again, they may also have negotiated a discount on these services.

Selling

Your property investment company should also have contacts with estate agents in the area and will be able to point you in the right direction to market and sell your property.

Chapter 4

Buying Off-plan: The Key Factors

From what you've read so far you will probably realise that there are certain key factors you should fully understand before investing in off-plan property.

I'll provide a brief summary of these in the sections that follow.

Mortgages

Make sure you understand:

- The difference between a residential and a buy-to-let mortgage. Interest rates are generally 0.5-1% higher for buy-to-let and there will also be a much larger deposit required from the lender (between 15% and 30%). The size of this deposit can increase even further if you are buying the property through a company.

- What shortfalls are and how they can dramatically affect the deposit you will be required to pay in order to get a mortgage. Shortfalls are created due to lower than expected rental valuations, lower property values or higher interest rates (or a combination of all of these factors). Shortfalls are explained in detail in Chapter 9.

- What is meant by the mortgage term 'Decision in Principle' – an initial confirmation that you will be granted a mortgage *in principle*. Note that a DiP is not an actual mortgage offer.

- The full costs involved in getting a mortgage in place, including survey fees, legal fees, lender's arrangement fees and mortgage broker's fees.

- The role of the surveyor with regard to the rental and property valuation required by the lender in order to achieve a successful mortgage offer.

- The different mortgage packages available and what fits your personal property goals the best. For example, do you want a fixed-rate mortgage that guarantees your mortgage outgoings for several years but comes with an early redemption penalty? Or do you prefer a variable rate mortgage with a lower interest rate and no redemption penalty but exposing you to the danger that interest rates may go up?

Discounts

Make sure you understand:

- Why a discount may not have any bearing on the amount of deposit required. In other words, just because a property is being sold at 15% discount does not mean the lender won't still require a 15% cash deposit from you.

- The difference between a genuine discount and a property whose price has been artificially hiked and then lowered in order to make a discount magically appear.

- No matter how big the discount is, the key number for a buy-to-let property is its rental value.

Legal Obligations

Make sure you understand:

- Exactly what your legal obligations are once you exchange contracts (or conclude missives in Scotland).
- Your liability should you have a new buyer in place but they do not complete on time or pull out of the deal.
- Exactly what will happen if you do not complete – will you be sued?

The Marketplace and How it Can Affect You

Make sure you understand:

- How over-saturation in the market can affect your ability to sell or rent your property quickly at the right price (if at all).
- How you need to be in a position to compete with other investors, for example by furnishing your property to a higher specification should you wish to rent it out, or reducing your price in order to get a quick sale.

The Surveyor

Make sure you understand:

- It's not your friendly neighbourhood letting agent or estate agent who puts the value of the property on your mortgage application – it is a surveyor acting on behalf of your lender.
- If the surveyor reduces the value of your property or its rental value or both, this could seriously affect the amount of

mortgage deposit you will be required to pay.

- If property prices *fall* after you exchange contracts you will still be legally obliged to pay the higher price.

The Solicitor

Make sure you understand:

- The importance of having a solicitor who is familiar with back-to-back transactions and/or assignable contracts should you wish to sell on to a new buyer.

- That the solicitor should ensure that the contracts/missives state the correct price (gross or net) required for your particular mortgage.

- Whether your solicitor requires a mortgage offer on exchange of contracts.

- That they are comfortable working with things such as gifted deposits, discounted properties and guaranteed rental schemes offered by the developer.

The Property Investment Company

Make sure:

- They are working for *you* and providing you with excellent service.

- All properties offered to you come with a RICS survey verifying the gross price (not the discounted price) and that you have a copy of this.

- There is an assessment of the rental potential of the property – with documentation.

- You are aware that no matter how large the discount is, and how good the deal sounds, you may still have to pay a deposit of 15% or more.

- You do your own 'due diligence' to ensure that the information you are being told is indeed correct (rentals in the area of interest are indeed £900 per month, not actually £550).

- You do not pay the property investment company its fee when you reserve a property but only when exchange of contracts takes place.

- You shop around. There are lots of property investment companies out there. Two per cent appears to be the average fee charged.

- You understand exactly what the property investment company is going to offer with regard to ongoing assistance and guidance (or if you are going to be dropped like a hot potato as soon as they are paid).

- You are aware of *all* the upfront costs associated with buying the property – not just a £500 reservation fee and £1,000 deposit on exchange of contracts.

Chapter 5

The Different Types of Off-plan Property

Off-plan investment can be broken down into several distinct categories:

SUBJECT TO PLANNING

The 'subject-to-planning' deal is the most speculative and arguably the most risky. It involves agreeing to buy property from a developer before planning approval has been received from a local authority.

Typically, the developer will have architects' drawings, estimated build costs and an idea of the price he would like to charge for the properties (probably based on similar properties in the area).

The benefit to the investor of reserving a property subject to planning is the long time lag. It may take up to six months or more for the developer to obtain planning permission. During this time the investor will benefit from any capital appreciation.

Warning

It is in your interests to only pay a nominal reservation fee prior to planning permission being obtained. To protect yourself and your wallet you should only exchange contracts and pay the deposit once planning approval has been granted. If this is not possible make sure your monies are paid into the bank account of the developer's solicitor (or, even better, your solicitor) and that the developer is unable to touch your funds until planning consent has been given. Reservation fees should also be paid into this account.

To profit from property deals like this, the investor usually needs to have a strong relationship with the developer and be able to buy a large chunk of the development. It is unlikely that an investor will be able to purchase just one unit from a developer subject to planning.

For this reason, it is usually property investment companies that negotiate this type of deal, passing the properties on to their clients.

It is important to understand that the property you initially reserved on may not be the same once it has gone through the planning process. I have seen one-bedroom apartments become two-bedroom apartments and vice versa. I have also seen apartments removed completely from the scheme!

You must therefore be prepared for prices to change as a result and you must also be prepared to end up with no property at all.

Make sure that it is agreed in writing that you are entitled to a full refund of your reservation fees if you are not prepared to exchange on an altered property.

Tip

Make sure you know when the 'stop end' date is for the developer to receive planning approval. This means that if planning permission is not received by a certain date all your money will be refunded. This date should be stated clearly in the relevant legal documentation.

If you are using a property investment company you should make sure that their payment is not due until planning has been granted.

Should the development not receive the go ahead or the property you want changes in some way, getting your fees back from some investment companies could prove extremely difficult.

Remember, sometimes planning may not be granted, and sometimes it could take a lot longer to achieve than anyone anticipated.

12 MONTH PLUS BUILD PROGRAMME

This is the route that most investors follow. It offers the security of knowing that all planning issues have been resolved and allows the investor to benefit from any capital appreciation while the property is being built and before major financial outlays and borrowings are required. There are dangers too, of course. When there is a longer-term build programme (lasting more than 12 months) investors have no way of knowing what the property market will be like when their unit is completed. Interest rates may have risen and rents and property prices may have fallen during this time. The investment climate can, of course, also change over a much shorter time period too.

Table 2
Pros and Cons of 12 Month+ Build Programmes

Pros:	Cons:
• Securing property at today's prices, resulting in capital profits if the market continues rising. • No mortgage to pay while property is being built. • Full deposit only required on completion. • Opportunity to sell the property in a 'back to back' transaction • Make a substantial profit if the market has risen during the build programme.	• Property prices may have fallen when the completion date arrives. • Mortgage deposit may be much more than you first thought if interest rates have risen and/or rental values and property prices have fallen. • The developer may go bankrupt, or put off building the property beyond the original completion date – all of which is out of your control. • The property market can change dramatically over 12 months.

BUYING OFF-PLAN IN AN EXISTING DEVELOPMENT

This route involves buying in the first, second, third or last phase of a development after it has been released to the general public. In small one-phase developments it involves buying a property much closer to the completion date.

The purchase is still off-plan, as the property has not yet been built, but the scope for capital appreciation is severely limited.

An investor purchasing at this stage would generally be looking to hold onto the property and rent it out rather than make a quick profit by selling it.

Alternatively the investor may still feel that he can sell it at a profit if he has bought at a genuine discount.

The advantage to the investor is that it is much easier to gauge the investment based on known facts rather than speculation. You will know what the interest rate for your mortgage will be and you will know the current rental value.

You will also be able to gauge the level of competition from other investors. Although the property may not have as much capital growth potential, you will have acquired a lower-risk and, hopefully, profitable property.

TIP

If there are a lot of properties in the area of a similar size and price for sale or to let, any discount you receive may be worthless. It is important to take into consideration over-saturation because if other people are having problems selling or letting then chances are you will end up in the same position.

THE OFF-PLAN RISK PYRAMID

The diagram below allows you to see, at a glance, the risk/reward spread involved in the different types of off-plan investment available.

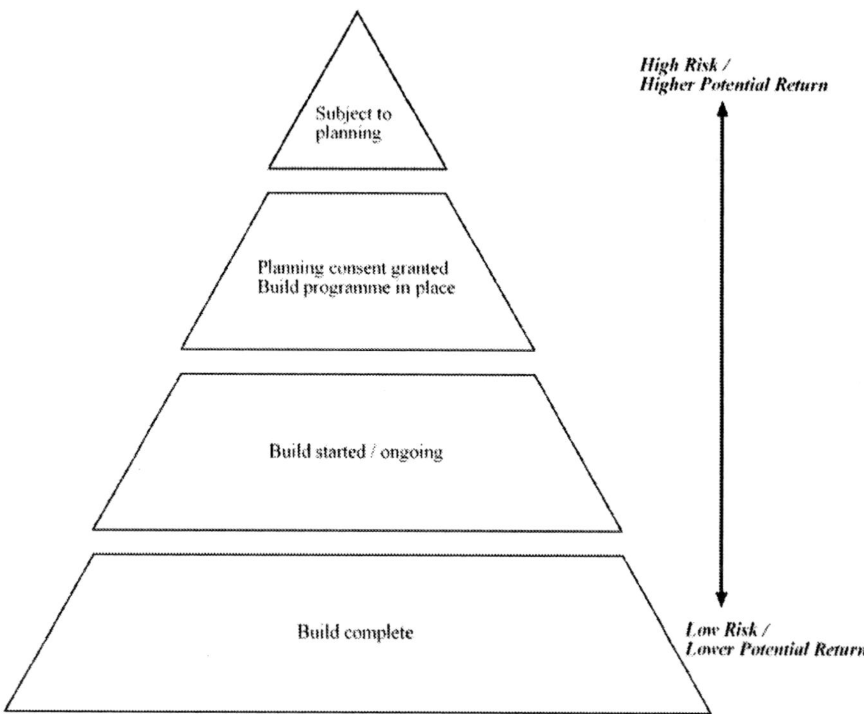

INVESTOR MENTALITY

When deciding how to go about investing in off-plan property you should take into account the very changeable nature of the property market, where events outside your control can have a negative impact.

The following are some of the questions you should ask yourself:

- Do I have a good financial safety net should the market change while the property is being built? For example, interest rates could rise, mortgage packages could change, and rental values and property prices could fall. All of these dangers are pretty much out of your control. The key is to have funds available to weather any potential storm.
- How much money can I afford to lose without harming my lifestyle?
- What type of investor am I: short-term, medium-term or long-term?
- Am I planning to sell or rent out the property? Am I prepared to change my goals should conditions in the property market change?
- Where am I interested in buying property: close to where I live, anywhere in the UK, or internationally?

Chapter 6

Off-plan Property Investment: The Risks

Many property investors ignore the risks. I guess we've all become accustomed to property rising by 10% to 20% per year or more. The sad truth is that property prices can go down as well as up.

Although there is little you can do to influence the financial landscape, by making well-informed decisions you can reduce your risks to a certain degree.

Property investors face different dangers to other investors and off-plan property investors have a whole range of additional risks to contend with.

HOUSE PRICE CRASH

One of the biggest risks facing buy-to-let investors is a property price crash. If prices fall far enough you could end up with negative equity: your property will be worth less than the mortgage over it.

At the time of writing prices in many parts of the country have fallen by a small amount and property is expensive according to most valuation yardsticks.

Even if there isn't a major crash it's important to remember that:

- Even if prices stay static for many years you could end up losing a lot of money. With inflation running at 2-3% per year, your wealth will fall every year in real, inflation-adjusted terms. For example, if you own a property worth £200,000 today and property prices stay static, in three years' time it will be worth just over £182,000 in terms of today's money.

And if the rental income from the property barely covers the mortgage and none of the other costs (maintenance, insurance, accountants fees and so on), your losses will be even greater.

- If prices fall by just a small amount it is your money, not the lender's, that will bear the full brunt of the fall.

- Come completion, your property may be worth less than when you exchanged contracts on it.

Example

Frankie buys a property for £100,000 using £15,000 of her own money and a buy-to-let mortgage of £85,000. Property prices fall by 3% over the next couple of years. As a result Frankie's property is now worth just £97,000. Due to personal circumstances she decides to sell the property and repay the mortgage. That leaves her with just £12,000 out of her original £15,000 – in other words, she has lost 20% of her personal money even though property prices have only fallen by 3%.

If you are a long-term investor and want to use your property investments to ultimately generate rental income, rather than capital growth, then a house price crash may not have much impact on you.

Indeed, during the last property crash of the early 1990s, many homeowners panicked, sold their properties and moved into rented accommodation. In some areas rental demand soared and landlords were laughing all the way to the bank!

Savvy investors were quick to realise that prices would rise again and started snapping up properties. A large number of letting agents set up their businesses on the back of this fresh demand for rented accommodation.

Where one door closes, a window always opens! Smart investors always see opportunities in times of crisis.

It's very difficult to predict what will happen to property prices over the next few years. In 2003 financial pundits were predicting a massive property price crash, arguing that prices could fall by as much as 30%.

Despite all the doomsday talk, property prices continued rising.

In some parts of the country property values have arguably risen to unsustainable levels. However, unlike the 1980s where almost 80% of the average person's disposable income was eaten up by mortgage payments, today that figure is only 25%.

Some off-plan investors, particularly those facing very long build times, could be severely affected by any fall in property values. The price you agree to pay when you exchange contracts is the price you will be forced to pay when the property is built.

If prices have fallen when you come to apply for your mortgage, you will have to make up any difference out of your own pocket.

For example, imagine you commit to buying an off-plan property for £100,000. Eighteen months later, when the property is complete, the world has gone into recession, stock markets have collapsed and property prices have fallen by 20%.

Your property is now worth £80,000 but you are contractually obliged to buy it for £100,000. Not only do you have to make up the £20,000 deficit but you may also have to put in the 15% deposit required by the lender!

This example may be a little extreme but only a fool would argue that property prices only go up!

A fall in property prices, even a modest fall, is one of the major risks of off-plan property investment and there's very little you can do about it.

One solution is to only buy off-plan property where the build programme lasts for just a few months. This will reduce the risk of losing money if property prices fall but will also limit your ability to make any meaningful short-term capital profits.

INTEREST RATE INCREASES

Off-plan property investors can also be hit hard if interest rates rise while their properties are being built.

For example, a rental income of £595 per month is enough to cover a £100,000 buy-to-let mortgage if the interest rate is 5.5%, with 130% coverage. However, if interest rates rise by just 0.25% you have to earn rental income of £623 per month to satisfy the same buy-to-let mortgage rules.

Remember most lenders insist that your rental income is 25-30% higher than your monthly mortgage payments.

If this is unachievable you will have to make up the shortfall by paying a higher deposit.

Remember, purchasing a property from plan often involves a long wait until the property is completed. Interest rates may have gone up several times since you initially did your figures and decided to invest.

Although most lenders want a deposit of 15% it could end up being substantially higher if interest rates have gone up.

Can this happen in practice? The answer, sadly, is 'yes'. In July 2003 interest rates were cut to 3.5%, pushing the cost of borrowing to its lowest level since the early 1950s. However, interest rates then rose five times to 4.75%.

Although 1.25% may not seem like much, when applied to a buy-to-let lender's mortgage criteria the impact can be quite devastating.

Unfortunately, it is very difficult to predict where interest rates or rental values are going to be when it comes time for you to complete on a property. You therefore have three choices:

- Avoid off-plan property with a long-term build programme – the longer the build, the more chances there are for changes in interest rates and rental values.

- Invest in property with a long-term build programme but be prepared financially for a change in the investment environment.

- Invest in property with a long-term build programme and keep your fingers, toes and other body parts crossed that interest rates don't go up, rental values and house prices don't go down, and you won't be caught short!

RENTAL VALUES FALL

Most buy-to-let mortgages are based on the property's ability to perform – in other words, the rental income it can achieve. Buy-to-let mortgages generally require the rental income to be 25-30% higher than the monthly mortgage payment.

For example, a property purchased for £118,000 would typically require a mortgage of £100,300 with a 15% deposit paid. With a 5.5% interest rate, a normal interest-only monthly mortgage payment would be about £460. Add 30% to this, and the lender will expect the property to earn rental income of £598 per month.

Imagine that you invest off-plan in a property in an area where the rental market is buoyant and £598 per month is easily achievable.

However, 18 months later, when the property is complete, an erosion of confidence in the housing market coupled with a glut of properties coming into the rental arena from investors has driven the achievable rental income down to £515 per month.

"Not a problem," you might say, "I can make up the difference out of my pocket, it is only £80". Not so. With a rental income of only £515 per month you could only expect to raise a mortgage of about £86,400 and will have to fund the difference yourself.

Added to this, interest rates may also have risen during this time, compounding the problem even further. Although this point has been made several times already in the book, it needs to be drilled into every property investor's brain!

The difference of £80 a month in the example above would actually require a further deposit of £13,900 from the investor on top of the 15% deposit they are already required to put in. This adds up to a whopping £31,600!

Make an appointment with a mortgage broker or lender in order to discuss this possibility before committing yourself to buy any property.

THE DEVELOPER GOES BUST

One of the most frequent questions I get asked is: "What happens if the developer goes bust before the property is completed. Will I get my money back?"

Unfortunately, the answer to this is very likely to be "No".

Thankfully, this is something I have not yet had to deal with, and I hope I never have to.

Generally, as an off-plan investor, you will have paid a deposit ranging from 5% to 10% of the purchase price to the developer when exchange of contracts takes place.

This deposit may be used by the developer to help fund the build costs and to provide evidence of sales to the bank, thus releasing more funding for further development. It also shows the developer that you are committed to the deal.

The sum you have paid to the developer can be quite substantial (for example, £25,000 on a £250,000 property) and could be tied up for as much as two years.

If the developer goes bust it's extremely unlikely that you will ever see any of your money again. As far as creditors go you will probably be very far down the pecking order.

You can possibly minimise this risk by doing some research on the developer: Do they have a good reputation, have they been around for a long time, do you know anyone else who has bought from them?

Find out what other developments they have worked on and go and visit them and inspect the build quality.

Only if you are completely happy should you part with your money. You may find that the developer has set up a company specifically for the development they are currently working on. This minimises their risk but increases yours.

Speak to estate agents in the area to find out if they know anything about the developer. Also find out who the building contractor will be. In many instances these days the developer does not do the building work but sub-contracts it out.

Therefore, the workmanship of the building contractor and ability to keep to deadlines should also be looked into as well.

SKY-ROCKETING BUILD COSTS

This is a situation I have come across several times. The developer sets a budget, does its costing exercise and then prices the properties accordingly.

In a few cases, where the properties have been reserved far in advance of being built, the building contractors may come back to the developer and tell them that due to an increase in the cost of materials or demand for their services, their fee has to go up.

If the development was sold in a more traditional way (not so far in advance) the developer would have the opportunity to increase the price of the properties prior to releasing the development to the general public.

There are many reasons why this situation may arise. An increase in oil or steel prices could affect the builder's costs or the developer could fall out with the builder and end up having to pay a higher price for a replacement.

The result, however, is generally always the same: the developer will try to charge you more for your property.

What happens next depends on what stage of the purchase process you find yourself. If you have only reserved the property, then there is no legal contract between you and the developer and you can simply cancel your reservation.

They may or may not return your reservation fee – holding on to it to cover 'administration' expenses is a possible outcome.

Alternatively you'll be 'offered' the property – but at the higher price.

If, however, you have exchanged contracts with the developer, you could find yourself in a stalemate. The developer can no longer afford to build your property at the agreed price and you do not wish to pay any more. The developer may then do one of the following:

- **Sit on the contract.** The developer might decide to wait and not do anything with the site. There may be a clause in the contract that states that if no work has started within a certain time the contract becomes null and void. At the end of this period, the developer may or may not return your exchange deposit to you.

- **Return your money.** The developer might just return your money, hoping that you don't take any legal action, and re-sell your chosen property to someone else at a higher price.

- **Sell the site and your contract to another developer.** Using this tactic, the developer shifts any responsibility to another company. The new developer may be able to complete the build at a reduced specification. This is no guarantee that your property will be built; the new developer may very well try the same tactics.

Ultimately, you will find yourself in an undesirable position. There is very little you can do to minimise this risk apart from researching the developer.

Speak to your solicitor and make sure that the title deeds are registered as soon as you exchange contracts. This means that the developer will not be able to sell the property on because it will be your name that appears on them.

Prior to exchanging contracts, ask your solicitor what will happen if this situation arises. If possible, see if a clause can be inserted in the contract to protect you.

THE DEVELOPER SELLS THE SITE TO SOMEONE ELSE

I have, unfortunately, experienced this on three separate occasions. After a developer has accepted reservations from clients, another developer offers to buy the development.

Faced with the chance of making a quick buck without having to get its hands dirty, the original developer sells the site on without any recourse to those who reserved a property.

This is one of the risks involved in buying property off plan!

Thankfully, more often that not, the developer will return any monies paid, but you may end up losing out on a good investment opportunity.

Our company sourced approximately 40 apartments from an established developer in an area that was just about to boom. Reservation fees were paid, contracts were exchanged and the completion date was approximately two years from the date of exchange.

Despite our rigorous due diligence we later discovered that the developer was having difficulty finding a contractor. The build costs on which they had based their prices were out to the tune of almost £700,000!

They claimed that this was due to a rise in oil, steel and labour prices. We reckoned they simply added up their numbers wrong!

Our clients had exchanged contracts and paid a 5% deposit. Property in this city had risen by almost 30% in 18 months and many of our investors were terrified at losing out on such a great investment opportunity.

Fortunately, the title deeds had been registered in the names of our clients. This limited what the developer could do with the site.

The properties were supposed to be completed in the summer of 2005. By the autumn of 2004 there was still no activity on the site. Not only that, the developer was becoming very difficult to contact by telephone or by email.

In late 2004 our clients received a letter from the developer stating that it was not going to proceed with the build and asking them to sign a piece of paper releasing their names from the title deeds.

We were not going to allow our clients to be treated in this way. They had paid the developer a reservation fee of £1,000, a deposit of 5%, solicitor's fees, mortgage broker fees and our fees. The fact that nothing was being built was the developer's fault.

Over many months, our clients' solicitor successfully negotiated for the developer to return all the reservation fees, solicitor fees, mortgage broker fees, our fees and their 5% deposits with interest.

The good news is our clients were not out of pocket. The bad news is they lost out on a great opportunity to make a quick 30% profit.

No doubt we will see the same site on offer through the usual property investor channels. I for one will be avoiding it.

SATURATION

Investing in property off plan can be a dream opportunity. By putting down just a small sum of money you can enjoy all the capital appreciation that occurs while the property is being built.

Unfortunately many greedy property developers and property investment companies have jumped on to the buy-to-let bandwagon in recent years. Nowadays a lot of new property built is sold solely to investors.

It seems that almost every spare piece of land is used these days to erect a new block of flats! Some seem to be built in the middle of nowhere, far from decent shops, schools and other amenities.

As a result, there is now a glut of certain types of property in some parts of the country. This means investors will have to reduce their prices if they want a quick sale. Alternatively they will have to hang on to them and rent them out... often at a reduced rental.

Investors can create an unsustainable property bubble in certain areas. If a development sells out quickly it may convince other investors to buy property in the area which in turn convinces other developers to build more property.

This can create an unsustainable 'investor-developer cycle'. The question investors should really be asking is whether there is demand from end-users: tenants and homeowners. If there is no realistic letting or sales market, then investors can find themselves sitting on a very expensive white elephant.

YOU BUY AT THE WRONG PRICE

It's a sad fact but there are some unscrupulous property developers and property investment companies out there.

That's why it's important to do your research and find out what comparable properties cost in the area.

It is essential to get a survey carried out before you reserve a property or, failing that, before you exchange contracts.

A survey will help you decide whether any discount being offered is genuine or not. For example, if a property investment company offers you an apartment for £130,000, discounted from £150,000, a survey will soon give you a good idea as to whether the property is really worth £150,000.

If you don't get a survey you may be in for a nasty shock.

HOW TO MINIMISE THESE RISKS

If you are buying an off-plan property by yourself, ask your mortgage broker to instruct a surveyor to value the property prior to reserving it to ensure the price the developer is asking is in line with the current market.

Ask to see the survey report and the comments that the surveyor makes. This will cost you just a couple of hundred pounds but could save you from making a costly mistake!

Ask the surveyor to give you a rental valuation and ask your broker if the market rent will cover the mortgage adequately.

Also ask the mortgage broker to calculate the level of deposit you will be required to pay if interest rates rise before the completion date.

Try to find out exactly how many developments are planned for the area and whether there is sufficient demand from people moving in to the area, students and so on. Go to the local planning authorities and find out how many developments are trying to obtain planning approval and where they are likely to be located.

Contact estate agents and letting agents in the area to find out how quickly properties are selling and what the level of rental demand is like in the area.

Find out if there are any new companies moving into the area or hospitals and the like being built which will create further demand for property.

Also find out what the average household income is in the area and whether that income would be sufficient to buy your property. Multiply the average household income by four (the average multiple that lenders will use to determine how much money they're prepared to lend) and see if that would entitle the average person to buy your property.

If it is too low you need to ask yourself who is going to be able to afford to buy this property (not to mention other properties in the development that other investors are selling).

These are all important questions that you need to ask before making any financial commitment.

One of the greatest misconceptions in the property industry is that whatever a developer is charging for a property is the value of the property. Ultimately a property is only worth what somebody is willing to pay for it.

COMMON FATAL ERRORS

There are a variety of errors new investors make when buying off-plan property:

Over-Buying. Many investors think that by purchasing properties that are due to complete at different times of the year they can use the profit from the sale of one property to fund the purchase of the next one, and so on. Unfortunately it rarely works this way. Buying property from plan exposes you to 'wandering' completion dates. To find a development that actually completes when the developer originally said it would, can be very rare.

Back-to-Back Transactions. Quite a few investors believe that they will never have to complete on a property – that they will simply sell it on prior to the completion date to a new buyer who will have to pay the deposit and other costs. You should never count on this happening – always presume that you will have to complete. If you do pull off a back-to-back sale by selling the property at a substantial profit prior to completion then congratulations! You have achieved the holy grail of off-plan property investment. But don't assume that this happens all the time. In fact, in the current property climate, transactions like these are becoming increasingly rare.

If you don't have the funds to cover all of the property purchase costs, including mortgage payments, stamp duty and legal fees then you may want to think twice about investing.

In fact, if you are planning on buying and selling this way, a word of advice: don't. It's too risky for the following reasons:

- New build properties can sometimes take on a life of their own as far as completion dates are concerned. Two properties I have purchased over the last couple of years have both run nine months overdue. Others have completed a month or two ahead of time. The upshot of this is that if you are planning on selling one property to fund the next, you may find yourself up the proverbial creek.

- Planning on selling a property for profit and actually having a sale go through are two very different things. Properties can sit unsold for many months (particularly in oversaturated areas, or if market conditions have changed). This will be disastrous if you need to free up funds to complete on another property.

- Selling a property and making a good profit are two very different things. You may walk away with just a few hundred pounds in your pocket at the end of it all.

Chapter 7

How to Choose the Best Off-plan Property

Knowing *what* type of property to buy and where are two of the most important decisions you have to make as a property investor.

If you're a long-term buy-to-let investor, it's essential to buy property that is very attractive to potential tenants. Without tenants there is no rental income and without rental income you won't be able to cover your buy-to-let mortgage.

Not only does there have to be strong rental demand in the area, rents should ideally be high enough to cover both your mortgage and the myriad of other costs you face as a landlord, in particular repairs and maintenance, furniture and appliances, insurance and letting agent fees.

Not all off-plan investors are able to achieve this goal for the simple reason that many new-build properties are often relatively expensive, resulting in high mortgage payments and low rental income.

The other critical factor is the property's ability to deliver capital growth.

Unless property prices are rising over the long term, buy-to-let investment is not going to make you any serious money. Because most of your rental income will be eaten up by mortgage payments and other expenses, the only way you can make a good 'paper' profit is if your property is rising in value.

If you're a short-term investor, wanting to sell as soon as the property has been built, capital growth has to take place over a very short period of time: months rather than years.

In the past it was possible for even novice investors to reserve any old off-plan property and make a quick profit by selling the property after it was built.

With property prices rising by 15-20% all over the country it was possible to make thousands of pounds profit out of almost any off-plan property in a short space of time.

'A rising tide lifts all ships', as the saying goes.

In today's property market, with property prices almost static, the only way to make a quick profit is to buy a property at a genuine discount or buy a property that is located in an up-and-coming area.

With prices rising far more slowly, investors are probably better off taking a long-term view and renting out their properties.

Properties with good investment potential can be found by:

- **Avoiding the lemmings.** Invest in areas that are up and coming and not saturated with other new-build properties or investors.

- **Avoiding wastelands.** Only invest in areas that have, or are soon to have, excellent infrastructure: good schools, good transportation links, hospitals, supermarkets and so on.

Achieving both these goals can be very difficult. When researching an area you should ask yourself:

- What other developments are planned for the area, potentially creating a glut of new-build properties?

- How robust is the current rental and sales market?

- How strong has capital growth been in the area over the past five years?

- What types of property are selling: for how much and how quickly?

- Are there any planned infrastructure improvements that could improve property values in the area?

- What is the average income in the area?

- Are there a lot of similar properties for sale/rent in the area? Could this be a sign of saturation?

One of the best ways to find out what type of property to buy and where is by speaking to local estate agents and letting agents. It sounds obvious but most investors don't tap into these invaluable sources of information.

Good estate agents know what type of property is selling well and for how much. Good letting agents know what type of property is in demand from potential tenants and how much they are willing to pay.

If a letting agent believes that the type of apartment you are buying will earn rent of just £500 per month, but your mortgage is likely to be £700, then you have a property deal that doesn't stack.

You can keep an eye on estate agents' shop windows or websites to see how quickly properties stay on the market. If they are really on the ball they will get in touch when they find out about any new developments that may suit your needs.

One of the best ways of finding a good agent and sorting the wheat from the chaff is by writing to them and seeing how quickly they respond. Ask them to send details about their company and see if they send something out promptly (if at all).

If they respond quickly they are more likely to be good at their jobs and good to you as a client.

FINDING YOUR PROPERTY

How do you go about finding property to buy before it has been built? I'm assuming here that you are investing alone and not using a property investment company. Property investment companies will help you find property... for a fee. More about these companies in Chapter 8.

There are many sources of information that will help you identify and locate possible off-plan opportunities. First of all you have to decide where to invest.

DECIDING WHERE TO INVEST

You need to have a complete understanding of the area in which you wish to invest. What is the economic outlook? Are jobs being created or lost in the area? Are there any major economic projects that could lead to increased demand for property?

If you live in a small town or village you are less likely to find any suitable investment projects than if you look in the nearest major conurbation – which may be many, many miles away from where you live.

Regardless of distance, once you find an area that takes your fancy, you need to research it thoroughly. Doing this will require time and effort but the more thorough you are the more you can alleviate some of the risks associated with off-plan investment.

The research you do should be exhaustive and detailed because should something go wrong you could end up losing a lot of money.

Speak to letting agents and find out what the going rate is for the type of property you are interested in buying – and find out how quickly properties are renting out in this area.

Speak to estate agents and find out what the approximate value is of the type of property you are interested in buying – and find out how fast they are selling in this area.

Call or visit at least three estate agents and three letting agents familiar with this area when you do this research and really pick their brains. You can be sure that each of them will tell you something worth knowing!

Find out if your area of interest is over-saturated with buy-to-let property, how much prices have gone up (or down) in the past six months and, most importantly, find out if they think there is still demand for property in this area.

If so, what *type* of property is in demand: it could be three-bed terraces, not two-bed apartments.

What is happening in the area to support further potential capital growth:

- Are there regeneration programmes in place that will lead to a rapid increase in property prices?
- Do any new or large national companies have plans to open in this area?
- What is the surrounding infrastructure like?
- Are there any universities in the area?

The UpMyStreet website (www.upmystreet.com) holds a wealth of information about various areas with regard to crime, unemployment, education, household income and average property prices.

You can also find out what the neighbourhood is like from an Acorn profile that has categories such as 'Wealthy Investors' through to 'Impoverished Pensioners'. Although you shouldn't base your decisions solely on these reports, they do help to give a broader picture of the area. You can access the Acorn profile by going to www.caci.co.uk/acorn.

REGENERATION AREAS

Regeneration areas hold a wealth of opportunities for the savvy investor, provided the price is right when you buy. Generally, the earlier on in the regeneration, the better the prices.

Regeneration areas are often areas of decay, both socially and physically. It takes time to get these areas back on track. If you purchase in a regeneration area right at the start, you may find that there are still problems with anti-social behaviour, dilapidated buildings and so on.

However, because the prices are generally lower, the rental incomes required are also lower. The upshot of this is that finding tenants tends to be easier as the properties are more affordable.

For some investors taking on properties in areas like this may be out of the question. However, many landlords (including many wealthy landlords) do very well out of lower priced properties, as they tend to have much higher rental yields.

It's a sad fact but many landlords find it untenable to take on DSS and other low-income tenants, fearing vandalism and other problems.

Having said this, as more developments are built, and the area is regenerated, property prices can rise phenomenally.

Bridgeton in Glasgow is a perfect example of just such an area. A few years ago, investors were buying properties in one development there for under £40,000. The latest units have now sold for £115,000.

At the time the area would not have been considered particularly 'desirable', as it was close to some run-down areas. However, the situation has improved.

Parking was provided, the properties are located close to a park, the city centre, and the city's universities and, on top of this, the apartments were more spacious and much more affordable than city centre units.

All in all, it is a desirable area due to location and the size and price of properties. And to top it off, rumour has it that the next development in the area will be starting at £140,000 a unit!

Overall, you have to ask yourself why is this an area that will grow in value and will be highly sought after by tenants or property buyers?

Don't be lured by any discount or because you like the look of the show property. You need to have a business approach to the development and understand the area and all its pros and cons.

After you have done all your research, found a property you are comfortable with and have had a survey carried out to ensure that the price of the property is reasonable and you are happy that there will be no over-saturation, you can decide whether to invest or walk away.

OTHER RESEARCH TOOLS

There are many ways you can find off-plan investment opportunities:

- **Drive around.** See if any developer signs have appeared advertising new sites. If you have chosen to invest in your local area, or nearby, then you should have a good idea as to where new developments are likely to be situated.

- **Local papers & property magazines.** There are a plethora of new developments and 'coming soon' sites listed.

- **Local planning offices.** Ultimately, these are the places that you will be able to find out what developments have applied for planning and which developments have obtained it. Most local authorities now have this information available on their websites.

Having said all of the above, many investors find it very difficult to source developments that are not yet available on the open market thereby giving them access to possibly the best deals.

This is where property investment companies come into play, as they are often approached by developers who want quick sales.

Any one investor may find it difficult to get a developer to agree to sell them one or two units prior to general release. They will also find it difficult to negotiate a discount.

Chapter 8

Benefits and Drawbacks of Property Investment Companies

Property investment companies offer the following benefits to investors:

- Discounted property
- Research, and
- Useful contacts and preferential rates

Let's take a closer look at each of these benefits in turn:

DISCOUNTED PROPERTY

When you buy off-plan property through a property investment company you will almost always be offered a discount – typically around 15%.

In other words, you will be offered a property for £85,000 that would normally cost £100,000.

How are property investment companies able to offer these discounts? Like everything in life, the more you buy of something the cheaper it gets.

If you go to a supermarket and buy toilet paper, you'll pay less for one of those 'multi packs' than if you buy a single roll. It's exactly the same with property – the more you buy the cheaper it gets.

Just imagine you're a property developer and an investment company with a big database of clients comes knocking on your door, offering to sell every unit in your new apartment block.

As a result you'll save thousands of pounds in advertising and other marketing costs and you'll be able to sell the properties much faster than expected. If the project is in its initial stages you will also be able to use these early sales to procure finance from a bank to complete the development.

In return for all these cost savings and other benefits you will probably be happy to charge a bit less for the properties.

That's how off-plan property discounts work. At least, that's how off-plan property discounts work *in theory*. In reality, you have to tread with care because many discounts are not genuine.

Remember that in return for finding you a property the investment company will want a fee – usually 2% of the property's price. So you have to make sure you are getting value for this money – in other words, a genuine discount.

In my opinion, you should always adopt the 'guilty until proven innocent' approach – always assume that a discount is NOT genuine until someone proves otherwise.

Here are some examples of discounts that are not worth having:

- **Phoney discounts.** Some developers (and property investment companies) raise the prices and then lower them, conjuring discounts out of thin air. For example, if the developer would normally sell a property for £170,000 he may raise the list price to £200,000 so that he can offer a 15% 'discount' and still sell the property for £170,000. Sounds unbelievable but it does happen.

- **Worthless discounts.** Sometimes property investment companies will offer an 'exclusive discount' but in reality you could probably get the same discount by approaching the developer directly. In these circumstances there's no point paying the investment company several thousand pounds in fees because anyone can get the same discount.

- **Genuine discount on over-priced property.** A lot of property developers simply charge too much for new-build properties. The prices of many off-plan properties are a lot higher than existing comparable properties. What this means is that, if you try selling your new house or apartment, you may struggle to get what you paid for it.

  In this situation any discount is not worth having because your property will probably still be worth no more than what you've paid for it.

- **Genuine discounts in an over-saturated area.** Developers may be desperate to get rid of standing stock. They may be offering massive discounts in order to shift them. The question you need to ask yourself is: if they can't sell them, could you? And why would you want them? However, it could simply be the developer's year end and the property could very well be in high demand for rental – obviously well worth researching to find out whether there is a bargain to be had or just a dud!

If a property investment company offers you a £100,000 property for £85,000 *and* only clients of the property investment company are entitled to receive the discount *and* the property is valued at £100,000 by an independent chartered surveyor, the property *may* then be worth buying

I say 'may' because survey values are not always accurate. Because every property is different you'll only find out what yours is really worth when you try to sell it.

Surveyors are human beings not machines and they all have different opinions as to a property's true value. Sometimes these will vary by as much as 20%.

So even if the property is valued at £100,000 by a respectable surveyor you may still only be able to sell it for £85,000, especially if the market is very quiet or there are lots of properties for sale in your area.

This brings me to another important point about discounts offered by property investment companies.

Some companies will end up selling most if not all the properties in a development. If there are lots of property investors trying to sell their properties or find tenants at the same this could have a negative effect on prices and rentals.

Make sure your chosen investment company tells you what percentage of properties is being sold to investors in your chosen development.

Discounts vs. Capital Growth

You should never buy a property simply because you can get it at a discount. Everyone loves a bargain but there are far more important factors to consider when buying property, one of the most important factors being capital growth potential.

Example

Joe pays £85,000 for a property valued at £100,000. He doesn't know much about the area and its growth prospects but is attracted by the £15,000 discount. Let's say he holds on to the property for 10 years during which time it grows in value by 5% per year. After 10 years he will have a property worth £163,000 – a profit of £78,000.

Joe's friend Stewart also pays £85,000 for a property but he doesn't receive a discount – in other words, he pays £85,000 for a property worth £85,000. Although he doesn't get a bargain he is far more choosey about where he invests. After doing a lot of research he buys his property in an up and coming part of the city and his property grows in value by 7.5% per year. After 10 years he will have a property worth £175,000 – a profit of £90,000.

This is an interesting result. Both investors paid £85,000 for their properties but only Joe got a discount. Despite this his friend Stewart ends up with £12,000 more profit because he was more careful about where he invested.

The moral of the story is don't be lured by discounts. If you're a long-term investor what really matters is rental income and long-term capital growth potential.

GUARANTEED RENTAL INCOME

Instead of providing a discount, some developers now offer guaranteed rent. The idea is that you don't have to worry about finding tenants to cover your mortgage because the developer will pay you money each month for a period of, say, three years. Alternatively, they may give you a lump sum on completion.

Sounds great but you have to be cautious and, as with every property investment, look at the whole picture. In many cases the developer may have simply raised the price of the property to cover the cost of the guaranteed rental payments.

If the property is found to be overpriced you may have difficulty getting a mortgage for the usual 85% of the price paid.

There are, however, rental guarantees that are worth having. For example, I know of one investment opportunity in Italy, where the developer has an agreement with a luxury holiday company to get wealthy holidaymakers to come and stay in the properties. The properties have not been hiked artificially in price and there most likely will be people renting the properties out throughout the year.

If you are offered a 'guaranteed rental scheme' it is important to understand where the rent is coming from, who is guaranteeing it and the way the whole deal is structured. Is the developer guaranteeing the rent simply by increasing the price of the property and paying the money back to you? If this is the case then I would probably steer clear.

RESEARCH

Where a property investment company can be very useful is if you want to broaden your investment horizons and invest outside the area where you live.

If you go it alone you may find it difficult and time-consuming doing the necessary research. A good property investment company will do the legwork for you, contacting local estate agents and letting agents, analysing the demographics of the area and past performance of property prices.

A good property investment company will also find out if there are other new developments in the area, when they are likely to be completed and how much they will cost.

In particular, the investment company should be trying to find out if the local market for new-build properties is becoming over-saturated.

A good investment company will commission an independent RICS survey which will be available for you to review. It will also provide, in writing, rental estimates from at least two local independent letting agents confirming the likely achievable rental income for similar properties. It will also want you to have a Decision in Principle from a mortgage provider.

All this research should be put into a concise, easily digestible report for you to read.

The quality of research on offer should form a major part of your decision when choosing a property investment company.

Furthermore, a good property investment company will only offer property that has passed a variety of quality-control tests. Over the years my company has turned away numerous developments for various reasons including:

- Rental income too low to cover a buy-to-let mortgage.
- Prices artificially inflated and then reduced to create the illusion of a discount.
- Local area over-saturated with properties for sale and to let.
- Valuations performed by a qualified surveyor show that the properties are overpriced.

Although research provided by a property investment company can be very useful you should not lose sight of the fact that they are in the business of selling property. In other words, the advice you receive may not be totally impartial.

So it's always a good idea to perform your own due diligence before committing to any purchase.

USEFUL CONTACTS AND PREFERENTIAL RATES

Property investment companies have a variety of valuable contacts to help you along the way, including mortgage brokers, estate agents and letting agents, snagging and furnishing companies and possibly even IFAs (Independent Financial Advisers) to assist you with other investment options, such as SIPPs (Self-invested Personal Pensions).

These contacts could be extremely useful if you are investing in a new area where you do not know local tradesmen or property service providers.

Furthermore, due to their size and the number of individuals they represent property investment companies can often negotiate preferential rates for their clients.

For example, a letting agent may charge between 10% and 15% commission per month. A property investment company with 20 or 30 properties in the area could probably negotiate to have this fee reduced to 7-10%. A letting agent would be foolish not to offer a reduced rate to get his hands on all that business because there's always someone else who will.

A property investment company can, through its size, negotiate reduced fees on a whole range of products associated with property investment, including:

- Mortgage broker fees
- Legal fees
- Professional snagging fees
- Furniture packages
- Letting fees

So for sheer money-saving potential alone, using a property investment company can be extremely beneficial.

DRAWBACKS OF PROPERTY INVESTMENT COMPANIES

Unlike IFAs and others in the investment industry, property investment companies are not regulated, so there is no official governing body (such as the FSA) to complain to if something goes wrong.

Recently, several companies that were found to be operating unethically were closed down by the Department of Trade & Industry (DTI).

One of the ways these companies worked was by asking investors for a lump sum – usually more than £50,000 – that would be used to build a property portfolio. The promise was to make you a 'property millionaire' within a year.

The upshot of the scam was that the directors spent all the money while feeding lie after lie to investors about the 'property' they had invested in.

If a property investment company wants to take money upfront so it can go off and 'invest' it for you, walk away. A good property investment company will only present potential investments to you, allowing you to decide whether you wish to proceed or not.

Many of the property investment companies around today sprung up between 2002 and 2003 as a direct result of their owners attending the various 'No Money Down' property investment seminars operating at the time.

Spurred on by tales of how easy it was to make millions of pounds from property in a relatively short space of time, these 'weekend investors' formed their own companies sourcing investment property for other people.

All they knew about property was what they learned from their weekend workshops. Would you trust your money to a company like this?

SHADY OPERATORS

A while ago there was a spate of stories about one particular property investment company that managed to get investors to part with lump sums of £20,000 to £30,000.

They would then 'wisely invest' this money in property in the north of England, often promising to create a portfolio of up to 12 properties for the investor.

Sadly it was a scam: the properties were derelict and even the insurance the investors were sold didn't exist.

The company was closed down by the DTI in 2003 but not before they conned someone I know out of £30,000 – almost all of her life savings.

Like many others she was simply desperate to get on the property ladder and this seemed like an easy way to do it.

The message here is that you should never believe companies that promise to make you a lot of money in a short space of time.

How else can you tell a 'good' property investment company from a 'bad' one?

A bad investment company will want its fees upfront, a good one is happy to wait until the deal is 'done' before requesting its commission.

A bad company probably won't be too concerned if you are able to complete on your property or not. After all, they took their fee at reservation and possibly may not have been in touch with you since.

A good company will also ensure that you have a Decision in Principle from a mortgage adviser before passing your reservation fee to the developer's solicitor.

A bad company will lure you in with promises of massive discounts. Whether these are genuine or not is another matter. Often either the developer or the property investment company itself will inflate the property price and then 'discount' it to make you think that you have got a great deal.

Very rarely will you see these prices backed up by a report from an independent RICS surveyor. I remember seeing one 'deal' from just such a company offering a 'massive 20% discount from market values'. They even had the audacity to publish a RICS survey to verify the discount.

Unfortunately for them, the RICS survey confirmed that the realistic values were several thousand pounds below their 'discounted' prices.

As mentioned previously, some investment companies will even buy the development themselves and then re-sell it to their clients, often failing to pass on the developer's discount to the client, or worse, raising the prices!

A bad company may very well cease all contact with you after reservation or exchange (except to maybe sell you more property!).

A good company will give you ongoing support and information from reservation through to completion and often beyond. It will liaise with your mortgage broker, your solicitor, furnishing companies and snagging companies and provide you with contact details for letting and estate agents.

PROPERTY INVESTMENT SEMINARS

Many property seminar companies will charge you thousands of pounds to attend their weekend property investment workshops.

Most then try to earn further fees by introducing you to specific property investment deals.

If you ask me that money would be much better employed as part of a deposit on a property, don't you agree?

The advice that most of these companies give is freely available.

DUE DILIGENCE

When choosing which property investment company to use, there are only three words I can say to you: research, Research, RESEARCH!

Go online and you will find hundreds of independent property investment companies. Go to their websites and see what they have to offer. In particular, see what properties they have on offer and what their business ethos is.

They all look pretty convincing, don't they? Slick, well presented, and professional. That's the problem with the internet: for just a few hundred pounds, even the most incompetent company can acquire a professional sheen with a well-designed website. The key in researching your chosen investment company is to cut through the glitz.

In order to earn your trust they should be providing you with reliable and trustworthy information that backs up your own due diligence in relation to the developments they are offering.

Your first port of call could be the Companies House website at www.companieshouse.org.uk where you can find out some information about the company: a list of its directors and shareholders and what other companies they are directors and shareholders of, how long the company has been going and the company's latest accounts.

I once saw a property investment company advertising on its website 'Established 1994' whereas their date of incorporation was actually 2003!

You can buy dormant companies that have been incorporated for many years and then change the name. If you can see any evidence of a name change, look for the date that happened: that will most likely be the date the company started.

Another way to find out how long the company's been going is to find out when its web address or domain name was registered.

You can do this by going to:

- www.networksolutions.com/whois – for .com domain names
- www.nic.uk – for .co.uk domain names

This isn't infallible because a company may have been going for some time but only registered its web address recently. Nevertheless it's a help.

Another invaluable source of information is online discussion forums. For those who don't know, a discussion forum is like a virtual notice-board where like-minded individuals get together online and 'post' questions, answers and opinions about a whole range of topics such as property investment.

There are thousands and thousands of discussion forums covering everything from aardvarks to zebras and many unmentionable subjects in between!

The best ones for property investment information include:

- Motley Fool – www.motleyfool.co.uk
- Singing Pig – www.singingpig.co.uk
- The Residential Landlords Association – www.rla.org.uk

All of these forums offer a search box into which you can type the name of a company and see if any comments have been made about it. This is a hit-or-miss way of doing research but if there are lots of negative comments alarm bells should start ringing.

Of course, comments made in forums should not always be trusted. Often the most vocal contributors are the ones with an axe to grind. So read the comments with an open mind and make your own decision.

You may also find articles and other information about the company by going on to one of the major search engines such as Google UK (www.google.co.uk) and entering the company's name.

Once you've done some background research it's time to get in touch with the company.

You may be tempted to ask to speak to one of the company's existing clients but don't be put off if they refuse. Rather, be encouraged.

Would you ask to speak to a client of Barclays Bank before becoming a customer? If you were signing up for a new doctor, would you ask to speak to current patients? Client confidentiality, patient confidentiality and data protection work against such disclosure.

A responsible investment company should be signed up to the Data Protection Act and should actively protect your personal investment details. If you ask to speak to an existing client and the company agrees, beware: you may be speaking to a sales person or a client on some commission structure.

Ask about their trading history: How many properties have they sold this year? How many properties did they sell last year? What are their criteria for sourcing property? Most importantly, ask how many developments they have turned away – a company that indiscriminately takes every development offered to it is showing no objectivity towards its clients' financial well-being.

Ask whether they charge a joining fee or whether they charge a monthly administration fee. If they offer free seminars or workshops, ask what the catch is – the free seminar is often a sales pitch aimed at signing you up to an expensive course.

Ask what their sales process is and how, and when, they take their money. If they take their fee at reservation or want it paid directly to them, be wary: you might not be able to get your money back if you decide not to proceed with a purchase.

Obviously, there are many reputable companies out there who may operate differently and take their fees upfront. They may well be very reliable, honest and trustworthy. Unfortunately, you may not know their business ethics until it's too late.

If you still cannot decide, visit their offices. The office environment can tell you so much about a company that mere research cannot reveal.

Type the address of the company into Google. This may reveal that they operate out of temporary serviced offices.

It is possibly better to deal with a company that has committed to a lease for several years as this may indicate that they plan to be around in five years' time! Again, it's not infallible but will help you build a picture about the company.

Even if the company is based far away from you, make the effort to visit them – by appointment, of course! Remember, this is your money so you have to know who you are dealing with!

I may be starting to sound like a broken record here, but I make no apologies for that. There are some very big and potentially costly issues to consider when using a property investment company:

- There is no regulatory body governing property investment companies.

- There are far too many investment companies that have literally set up overnight with their owners having little or no knowledge about the property industry.

- These companies try to attract clients who are, in many cases, lured by promises of becoming 'property millionaires'.

- Many of the investors buying through some of these unscrupulous companies should not be purchasing property at all. They don't understand how the market can dramatically change and they simply do not have the funds to ride out increases in interest rates or rental voids.

- Getting caught up in the sales hype can be a disaster. Don't believe for one second that your property is going to require little or no deposit or that you will be able to sell your property without having to arrange a mortgage. And if it's a longer-term build programme, what works today to make the deal stack may not work in 18 months' time.

Many property investment companies can be likened to used car salesmen: They are your best friend until you've bought the car and then, if anything goes wrong (which it often can), their commitment to customer satisfaction evaporates because they're too busy lavishing attention on the next 'punter'.

Rarely does buying a property go smoothly. There are always hitches along the way, and buying property from plan is no exception. Therefore, should you choose to work with a property investment company, you need to have one which will help you solve any hiccups you may experience.

A good property investment company is:

- Attentive
- Service oriented
- Helpful
- Approachable
- Hardworking, and ultimately
- Trustworthy.

Chapter 9

Financing Your Investment

As a rule of thumb I recommend having between 25% and 30% of the purchase price of a property available to cover the purchase costs. Always expect to pay some or all of the following expenses:

- Reservation fee
- Developer's deposit
- Mortgage deposit
- Mortgage broker's fee
- Lender's arrangement fee
- Conveyancing fee
- Survey fee
- Searches and registration fees
- Mortgage payments before the property is let/sold
- Council tax before the property is let/sold
- Buildings and contents insurance
- Furnishings
- Estate agent or letting agent fees and costs
- Stamp duty
- Snagging fees, if a professional snagging company is used
- Property investment company fees

Do not be fooled into thinking that investing off-plan is a quick and inexpensive way of making money out of property. Even though you may make a substantial profit when you sell, you may have to part with a significant amount of cash before that happens.

Always prepare for the worst possible outcome. For example, be prepared for the property to sit on the market for many months before you find a buyer or tenant.

Apart from using your own cash you will probably also need a buy-to-let mortgage. The rest of this chapter takes a detailed look at some of the key issues surrounding this type of mortgage and other financial issues affecting off-plan property investors.

USEFUL BUY-TO-LET MORTGAGE FORMULAS

Most buy-to-let lenders insist that the rental income from a buy-to-let property must be 25% to 30% higher than the monthly mortgage payment.

There are two important mortgage formulas you should understand:

- **The Maximum Mortgage Formula.** If you know how much rent a property will earn, this formula tells you how much the lender will be prepared to lend you and hence how much you should be prepared to pay for the property.

- **The Minimum Rental Formula.** If you know how much a property is likely to cost, this formula tells you how much rent you will have to earn to qualify for a mortgage.

Both formulas provide similar information. Which one you use depends on what information you have available. Let's take a closer look at each of these formulas in turn.

The Maximum Mortgage Formula

Let's assume the average rental income for similar properties in your area is £550 per month (£6,600 per year) and the interest rate on a buy-to-let mortgage is 5%. We'll also assume that the lender wants cover of 130%. In other words, for every £1 of your mortgage payments they want you to earn £1.30 in rental income.

The maximum the lender will let you borrow:

Rental income ÷ mortgage coverage x 12 ÷ interest rate

Plugging the above numbers into the formula:

£550 ÷ 130% x 12 ÷ 5% = £101,539

The result is the maximum amount of money you can expect to borrow. I say 'expect' because everybody's situation is different, which is why you should always speak to your mortgage broker or lender before committing yourself to buying any property.

What this formula will help you decide is whether the property in question is a viable investment. In other words, it will help you decide whether the property fits into your lender's criteria or if it is too expensive relative to the rental income it can generate.

It is worth remembering that this figure of £101,539 is just the amount you would expect to get from a lender. The full price you will be able to pay for the property, while keeping the lender happy, is:

£101,539 ÷ 85% = £119,458

The number 85% is used because most lenders are prepared to lend you, on average, 85% of the price you pay for a buy-to-let property.

Armed with this knowledge you know that if a property rents out for £550 per month you can afford to pay no more than £119,458.

The Minimum Rental Formula

Let's say you're interested in a property that costs £150,000. With a 15% deposit, the mortgage required will be £127,500. We'll assume interest rates are at 5% and the required rental cover is 130%.

To qualify for an 85% LTV mortgage the property must be able to generate a monthly rental income of:

Mortgage required x interest rate x mortgage coverage ÷ 12

Plugging the above numbers into this formula we get:

£127,500 x 5% x 130% ÷ 12 = £691 per month

In other words, the property has to be able to earn £691 per month to satisfy the lender's criteria. Are newly built properties in your chosen area renting out for this kind of money? If not, the property may not be a viable investment.

MORTGAGE SHORTFALLS

What if you discover that similar properties are renting out for only £600 per month? That's only £91 per month less than the figure in the above example. Surely you can make up the £91 per month out of your own pocket? Unfortunately you cannot!

If you go back to the first formula, the maximum mortgage formula, and plug in the monthly rental income of £600, you will see that the maximum mortgage you can get will be £110,769.

So if your chosen property costs £150,000, with a deposit of 15%, you will still have to put in *an extra* £16,731 on top of your deposit to cover the mortgage shortfall – a total sum of £39,231.

The Value of the Property

When you buy an investment property the lender will typically let you borrow:

- 85% of the *value* of the property, or
- 85% of the *price* you pay for the property,

whichever amount is the lower.

So if you agree to purchase a property for £200,000, which is valued at £220,000, the lender will typically give you:

£200,000 x 85% = £170,000

You will have to pay a deposit of £30,000 to make up the remaining 15%.

But what if you end up paying £200,000 for a property valued at just £190,000? In this case the lender will typically give you:

£190,000 x 85% = £161,500

You will have to pay a 15% deposit of £28,500 plus an extra £10,000 to make up the shortfall. Therefore, you would be required to come up with a £38,500 deposit.

The Rental Value of the Property

A major difference between residential mortgages and buy-to-let mortgages is that the lender is not only interested in the value of the property but its rental value as well. The lender wants to be sure that the rental income from the property will comfortably cover the mortgage.

Typically for every £100 of mortgage you pay, the lender wants you to earn £125 in rental income. In the jargon of the property business, they're looking for 125% rental cover.

And if your property doesn't earn enough rental income to cover a full mortgage, the lender will offer you a smaller loan and you will have to cover the shortfall out of your own pocket.

Example

Dave buys a flat for £125,000 and the surveyor assesses its rental value at £625 per month.

Dave intends to pay a deposit of £18,750 (15% of the purchase price) and hopes that he will be able to raise a mortgage for the balance of £106,250. Can he do this?

The lender Dave wants to use has a buy-to-let package with a 5% interest rate and requiring 130% rental coverage. The monthly mortgage payment will be:

£106,250 x 5% ÷ 12 = £443

Add the extra 30% rental cover to this and the figure rises to £575, well within the quoted rental value of £625.

The question is, how big a loan can Dave raise with a quoted monthly rental income of £625? Assuming the same 5% interest rate and 130% coverage requirement, then using the Maximum Mortgage Formula, Dave works out that he can raise a mortgage of £115,384.

This sounds great and Dave thinks that he might only have to pay £9,616 in deposits (£125,000 - £115,384). Unfortunately, as is often the case, the lender requires Dave to pay the full 15% deposit.

Now let's say that the interest rate is 6%. The monthly payment required will now be:

£106,250 x 6% x 130% ÷ 12 = £691

* ReadyReckoner:

This is above the quoted rental income and the lender will not be happy to provide the loan unless Dave increases his deposit to bring the loan amount down.

Although the difference is a modest £66 per month, it has a big impact on the amount the lender will allow Dave to borrow. Using the Maximum Mortgage Formula again, we can now see that the lender will allow a loan of only £96,154.

The difference between what Dave wants to borrow and what the lender is prepared to lend is a whopping £10,096. This is Dave's mortgage shortfall that he will have to pay *on top of* his 15% deposit.

The mortgage shortfall danger is something all investors have to be aware of. If their initial view on the rental value of the property is incorrect, or it alters, or if interest rates rise between agreeing to buy a property and having to make final payment, you may find you cannot get the desired level of mortgage.

If you would like to do your own mortgage shortfall calculations you can download a little program we developed ourselves to do these on the fly. We call it the Ready Reckoner and you can obtain a copy by going to: www.hattanandgrand.com/readyreckoner

UNDERSTANDING GEARING

If you have already bought your own home with a mortgage then you are a 'gearing expert' already!

Gearing involves using other people's money to finance your investments, while keeping all the capital gains to yourself.

If you've bought your own home you will probably have put in a relatively small percentage of the purchase price, perhaps 5%. Although you may actually 'own' just 5% of the property, all the capital growth over the years is yours.

For example, let's say you buy a flat in 2005 for £100,000, paying a deposit of 5%. So for a down payment of £5,000 you have secured an asset worth £100,000 with the lender financing the other £95,000.

By 2010 the property has risen in value to £130,000. So your initial £5,000 investment has delivered a gross profit of £30,000. That means your money has grown by a whopping 600%!

Here's a more involved example, this time using off-plan investment property.

Let's say you decide to invest in a property valued at £100,000. The property will be ready for completion in two years' time. On exchange of contracts you pay a deposit of £5,000 or 5%.

During the two-year build programme, the property rises in value to £115,000. It is your intention to sell the property back-to-back and make a quick profit on completion.

Sensibly, you arrange a mortgage to cover your back in case you cannot find a buyer in time. We'll assume this unfortunate situation arises and you have to pay a further 10% (£10,000) mortgage deposit on completion.

Let's also assume your other costs (legal fees and so on) come to 4% of the original value (£4,000).

Thankfully, you manage to get a quick sale and only have to pay two months' mortgage payments totalling £864 (mortgage of £85,000 at 4.69% with 130% coverage). You sell the property for £115,000, releasing the £30,000 equity in the property.

Your return on this property can be calculated as follows:

- Your costs to buy the property are your deposits of 15% plus your fixed costs of 4% plus two months' mortgage payments. This comes to £19,864.

- Of this, you'll get back your £15,000 in deposits when you sell the property. So your real costs are just £4,864.

- The growth in the property is £15,000, resulting in a gross profit of £10,136.

- This equates to a gross return on investment of 208.4%

There could also be stamp duty to pay, although not in this example as the price of the property is below the current £120,000 threshold.

This example shows that, despite the various costs, off-plan property, combined with gearing, can earn you a substantial return on relatively small investments.

UNDERSTANDING THE LENDER'S ATTITUDE TO RISK

Always remember that you carry all the risk when you borrow money to invest in property. The lender will almost always be safe, even if your property has to be repossessed.

Because lenders never hand over more than about 85% of the value of the property, even if property prices fall by 15% straight after you take out the loan, the lender can still repossess your property without losing a penny if, for example, you consistently default on your payments.

Even if you've repaid 75% of your loan, the lender is well within its rights to repossess the property and sell it – for whatever value – to recoup its money.

Hence that awful phrase: "Your home is at risk if you do not keep up the mortgage repayments on it."

TYPES OF MORTGAGES AVAILABLE

Most buy-to-let mortgages are interest-only mortgages. Many investors choose this type of mortgage because it is the most affordable and the easiest to fit into the lender's criteria.

As its name suggests, an interest-only mortgage requires that you pay interest only. You do not have to repay any of the original loan until the end of the mortgage term, possibly 25 years from now.

Because you do not have to repay any of the loan – just the interest – the monthly payments are much lower than for repayment mortgages.

For example, a typical interest-only mortgage for £100,000 will cost you £417 per month if interest rates are at 5%. A repayment mortgage will cost you £585 per month.

In the current market climate, with property prices high and rents relatively low, having the lowest possible mortgage payment is essential if you are a buy-to-let investor.

The lower your mortgage payment, the easier it is to cover all your other landlord expenses out of your rental income without having to dip into your own pocket.

Some lenders insist that you set up a parallel savings plan so you have enough money to pay off the loan at the end of the mortgage term. Most lenders, however, only recommend that you do this and, in practice, there are very few buy-to-let investors who do.

Instead they take the view that in 25 years' time the property will have increased in value significantly. At this point the property can be sold, the mortgage repaid and the investor can pocket the remaining profit. Of course, you may choose to do this at any time!

Those looking to sell property soon after completion should also make sure they avoid mortgages with redemption penalties or tie-ins. These levy high charges if you sell your property and pay back the mortgage within a short period of time.

DISCOUNTS AND MORTGAGES

Many property investors believe they will not need a mortgage deposit if they buy a property at a big enough discount: the lender will simply allow the discount to be used in lieu of a deposit.

Anyone who thinks this is in for a bit of a surprise. Most lenders now insist that a cash deposit is paid by the buyer and will ask your solicitor for proof.

As stated before, many lenders let you have:

- 85% of the *value* of the property, or
- 85% of the *price* paid,

whichever is the *lowest* amount.

So if you pay £100,000 for a property worth £120,000 the lender will only lend you 85% of £100,000, in other words £85,000.

NOTE: Mortgage packages are constantly being introduced, reviewed and withdrawn. It is important to speak with your mortgage broker to understand what type of package is available to you at any given time.

The other important point to remember about discounts is that even if the property is being offered at an attractive discount, if the rental income is too low to adequately cover the mortgage payments, you are still going to have to inject extra cash to make up the mortgage shortfall.

Here's an example that shows how a large discount could be immaterial to the viability of an investment.

I was recently offered properties in an off-plan development in Manchester where there was an incredible 25% discount! I carried out my initial research and was satisfied that the discount was indeed genuine.

However, there were some problems with this investment opportunity:

- The discounted prices started at £390,000.
- The highest rental income that could be achieved in the development was around £900 per month – a rental yield of just 2.77%.
- In order to rent out the properties they would need to be furnished to an extremely high specification, costing a further £10,000 to £15,000.
- The development was due to be completed in a month, giving no scope for capital appreciation and little time to sell on in a back-to-back transaction.
- At these prices there would be a limited market to sell to, so the properties would most likely stay on the market for quite some time. Perhaps that's why the developer was offering a 25% discount!

So I reached for my mortgage shortfall calculator and put in the figures:

Interest rate: 5.69% (the lowest rate at the time)
Rental coverage: 130%
Purchase price: £390,000

The rental required to service a mortgage on this property with an 85% mortgage was a staggering £2,043 per month! This was a far cry from the quoted figure of £900.

So I turned the equation around to see how much I could borrow with a rental income of £900 per month... a paltry £146,005. This meant that if I purchased the property I would have to make up a jaw-dropping shortfall of £185,495 on top of my £58,500 deposit!

That's right, I would have to come up with an extra £185,495 in cash in order to secure just one unit, as the lender would only be prepared to offer a mortgage of £146,005 based on the rental income of £900 per month.

So you can see that the 25% discount, although genuine and very generous, really had very little bearing on the viability of the investment.

So to recap, it is not so much the size of the discount that will help you obtain a buy-to-let mortgage with 'little or no deposit' – it is actually the rental valuation. And it is your lender's surveyor who decides upon the rental valuation, not your friendly letting agent.

Obviously, the example above is for a property that has quite a considerable price tag attached to it. However, the theory is the same for any property. If the rental doesn't meet the lender's coverage criteria, then there will be a shortfall and that shortfall will have to come out of your pocket.

Having said all this, a genuine discount is still extremely attractive. After all, everyone likes buying something for less than it's worth! A discount on an off-plan property can be beneficial for the following reasons:

- It creates further equity in the property. If the property is purchased from plan, the discount plus any capital growth during the build programme can equate to a substantial profit for the investor.

- It reduces the purchase price of the property, thereby making the required mortgage smaller and reducing the level of rental income needed to make the deal viable.

SPECIFIC FINANCE ISSUES FOR OFF-PLAN INVESTORS

As mentioned previously, there are several specific issues with regard to financing property bought from plan:

- **Interest rates rise** – Interest rates have gone up from the time when you initially reserved on the property. Where beforehand the investment was sound, you now find yourself in a position where you have to add funds on top of the 15% deposit you had budgeted for.

- **Rental values fall** – This will have the same effect as a rise in interest rates.

- **Property values fall from the time you reserved** – Oh dear. The lender will only offer a mortgage based on the property's current market value, not the price you're obliged to pay. So if you reserved a property for £100,000 but by the time you come to complete it is only 'worth' £90,000, you will still owe the builder £100,000. The lender will only offer a maximum mortgage of £76,500, meaning you will have to find £23,500!

Take some time to go through the Ready Reckoner and play with different scenarios: different rentals, interest rates and purchase prices. Then you'll have a thorough understanding of how one thing can affect another.

THE MYTH OF 'NO MONEY DOWN'

You may have seen the advertisements in the newspapers and magazines, heard them on the radio or had an unsolicited piece of mail through your letterbox – 'be a millionaire' using 'little or none of your own money'.

Statements like these are generally designed to lure in the gullible or desperate would-be investor and are in many cases misleading.

For the most part these statements are created by 'marketing executives' who have very little real understanding of the property market. In most cases, they are making their money from people who are desperate to get on the property ladder. It is often the case that the only people becoming millionaires are the owners of these companies!

Warning

A recent radio ad I heard spoke about a chap 'securing' almost £1 million of property thanks to a course he had been on. Well, I can 'secure' as much property as I want by paying small reservation fees. Whether I can raise an investment mortgage on those properties, or come up with the developer's deposit, is another matter altogether!

One of the reasons why there has been such a surge of interest in off-plan properties is because, for a while, some lenders were happy to accept any equity in the property (i.e. from the discount) in lieu of a deposit. At the time, with low interest rates and lower property prices in general, the deals stacked with the lenders' criteria.

Loan-to-value (LTV) buy-to-let mortgages, where the lender never requested details as to where the deposit came from, meant that many investors were, theoretically, able to utilise the discount as the deposit. These mortgage packages would allow you to raise an 85% mortgage on the value of the property. Therefore, if the value of the property was £100,000, but you were buying it for only £85,000, you would be able to raise an £85,000 mortgage - effectively 100% funding, provided the rental income stacked.

In a rising market, it was easy for lenders to bank on the value of your property going up. In a subdued or flat market, you will find it hard to find such mortgage packages available.

Many investors and investment companies started abusing the system by having the developers artificially inflate and then discount the property prices.

This meant that the property would show an incredible (not to mention, artificial) 15% discount, or more. In many cases, these companies and their investors were not even having independent surveys carried out on the properties in order to confirm whether the prices were in line with the current market values. The investors themselves didn't think twice about whether the discounts were genuine.

But even more importantly, what no one was really looking at was the rental income.

As it is the surveyor who will give the final report to the lender, detailing what rental income the property can expect to earn, the amount of 'discount' becomes irrelevant. Even with a 25% discount (as proved earlier in this chapter), if the rental was not providing at least a 25% profit margin after monthly mortgage payments, investors would still have to put in their own money on top of the required deposit to cover the shortfall.

This small, but immensely significant point seems to have been overlooked by many of these so-called property investment companies!

No money down schemes trumpet the glories of using 'Other People's Money' to build a property portfolio. However, you simply cannot buy a property without using some of your own money. Even if you have raised the deposit by re-mortgaging your home, you may find yourself with higher monthly mortgage payments. At any rate, the debt on your home is greater.

Even if you can avoid paying a mortgage deposit you will still have to pay conveyancing fees, stamp duty, survey fees and your lender's arrangement fees.

You will then have to foot monthly mortgage payments until you find a tenant or a buyer.

Furthermore, if you are an off-plan investor you will also have to pay the developer a deposit. Very few developers will allow you to reserve a property for a few hundred pounds without any further financial commitment until completion.

They want to see a commitment to buy from the investor. And therefore, they will almost always ask you for a deposit. That deposit may range from 5% to 10% of the purchase price, and they will want that deposit on exchange of contracts.

So suddenly 'No Money Down' becomes '10% deposit plus associated fees'. Doesn't seem such a great offer now, does it?

In my opinion you should stay away from property investment courses that push 'no money down' deals and use that money to buy property instead of lining OPPs (Other People's Pockets)!

The bottom line is this: If you cannot afford to pay a 15% deposit, plus another 2-4% for costs, *plus* have enough put by to cover six months' mortgage repayments, then you shouldn't be in this game.

Having said all of this, there are certain 'techniques' that can result in you ending up having to not put in very much money. Obvious techniques such as getting a bridging loan or using your credit card to pay for a deposit are not recommended as the interest rates are high and redemption penalties can be severe. Ultimately how you structure your purchase will be dependent on your goals – whether you are a short-term or long-term investor.

You could, for instance, immediately re-mortgage your property with a loan-to-value package to recoup your deposit. This would only be feasible if the rental income still covered your higher mortgage payments. You could re-mortgage your home releasing any equity in it to cover the deposit and any expenses. Depending on interest rates at the time, you may even end up reducing the monthly mortgage payments on your home. Effectively, this is 100% funding.

GIFTED DEPOSITS

A gifted deposit is a method of purchasing a property where the vendor gives, or 'gifts', to you the deposit for the property you are purchasing from them.

Builders sometimes give gifted deposits of around 5% or some other incentive (such as 'Stamp Duty Paid') on their new developments. Not all lenders accept gifted deposits and those that do generally only accept up to 5% (sometimes more if you are buying from a family member).

It also may be possible, depending on the lender's criteria and other factors, to use this 5% gifted deposit towards your overall deposit, thereby reducing your deposit commitments (remember, the developer will generally always require a deposit from you).

It is worth noting that the gifted deposit will go towards reducing the purchase price of the property and will not be cash in your hand. Depending on interest rates, rental income from the property, and the current value of the property you may also be able to re-mortgage and pull the gifted deposit, plus any equity, back out.

THE BUYING-TO-SELL MISCONCEPTION

If I only had a pound for every time I have heard people say to me, "But I am only buying to sell, not to let – so I won't need a mortgage", then I would be very wealthy indeed.

There are far too many off-plan investors out there who believe that they will not need to arrange a mortgage or that rental income doesn't matter because they are planning to sell their property before completion.

Do not be fooled: it is crucial to have a mortgage offer in place and to have enough funds available to cover all aspects of a property purchase, including having a financial safety net. Here's why:

- No deal is a done deal until it is finalised. Even though you may have lined up a new buyer for the property, until that buyer completes you are still financially liable for the property.

- You may not be able to sell the property until well after completion. If this happens then you will need to have a mortgage in place in order to complete and be able to service the monthly payments until you do sell it.

- Developers can pursue you for the debt and charge you interest if you fail to complete on time. I have heard of developers charging interest at rates as high as 8.75%, compounded daily!

- Don't assume that an end-user buyer will be as comfortable as you in purchasing from plan. Many will want to see, feel and touch exactly what they may be living in – once again, you may have to complete in order to sell.

As you can see, these are just a few of the more common examples of what could potentially go wrong in simply assuming that you will sell your property on in a back-to-back transaction.

Chapter 10

'A-Z' of Off-plan Buying Costs

As mentioned earlier, all property purchases are going to cost you money – there is no escaping that fact. Therefore, I thought it would be helpful to provide a general cost breakdown from start to finish for a new-build property so that you know what to expect and what to budget for.

RESERVATION FEE

Reserving a property is likely to cost you between £500 and £1,000. Find out if the reservation fee is refundable or partly refundable should you not proceed with the purchase. Check the reservation form for the refund clause – make sure that it states 'subject to contract' which means your fee will be refunded if you are not happy with an unreasonable clause in the contract.

The reservation fee will either be returned to you on completion or the purchase price will be reduced accordingly.

DEVELOPER'S DEPOSIT

To show your commitment to completing the purchase the developer will always require a deposit when you exchange contracts – even if the completion date is as much as two years away.

In England and Wales this deposit is normally a percentage of the purchase price, typically between 5% and 10%. In Scotland, where you 'conclude missives' you usually pay a fixed fee of between £1,000 and £5,000. Some developers in Scotland prefer you to pay a percentage of the purchase price.

In England and Wales, you will be expected to exchange contracts 28 days after reservation fees and forms have been submitted. In Scotland, you will be expected to conclude missives 14 days after your reservation fees and forms have been submitted to the developer.

MORTGAGE DEPOSIT

A second deposit is required on completion for the outstanding amount not covered by the initial deposit.

Lenders will view your initial deposit as part (or all) of the mortgage deposit required by you. Therefore, if you have an 85% LTV loan and you have already paid 10% to the developer on exchange of contracts, then you will only need to pay a further 5% to the lender (provided that there aren't any shortfalls).

Example

Steve and Sue invest in a flat for £150,000. When they exchange contracts they pay a 10% deposit of £15,000 to the developer.

They then arrange an 85% buy-to-let mortgage for £127,500. That still leaves 5% of the purchase price outstanding. On completion this money will have to be paid to the developer.

CONVEYANCING FEES

With off-plan property the conveyancing process is generally split into two parts:

- Reviewing the purchase contract and conducting searches.
- Completing the transaction.

If your property has a long build programme, make sure your solicitor's fees are divided in two so you don't have to pay now for a service that may only be carried out in a year or two's time.

Listed below are types of search that should be carried out:

Pre-Exchange Searches

- **Local authority search** – this is to check if any new developments are planned near your property. Expect this search to cost between £85 and £125.

- **Water authority search** – this is to check the local water and sewerage infrastructure. Expect to pay between £15 and £30.

- **Environmental Search**. May be required, particularly for newer properties. Expect to pay upwards of £30.

Pre-Completion Searches and payments

- **Company search.** Occasionally required on a purchase from a limited company. Approximately £20.

- **Bankruptcy search.** £2 per name. Required on behalf of the lender to check if the buyer has ever been declared bankrupt.

- **Land registry search.** Identifies any mortgages to be repaid by the seller. Cost £4.

Post-Completion Payments

- **Land Registry Fees.** The charge for registering the title of the property under your name. A charge is made for issuing a Land Registry Certificate that is a copy of the entry in the database. Fees vary according to the price of the property and are in the region of £60 to £250.

It's important to note that if you are using a property investment company you will generally be required to use the solicitor nominated to act on behalf of everyone investing in the development.

Developers prefer working with one solicitor who acts on behalf of all clients, instead of 20 solicitors acting for individual investors.

The solicitor should always lay out his scale of charges in writing to you before any work is done.

If you are planning on selling your property, this will result in extra legal charges.

MORTGAGE BROKER'S FEE

You only pay this fee if you use a broker to arrange your mortgage but not all of them charge for their services. Those that do generally charge 1% to 1.5% of the purchase price of the property.

You shouldn't use a broker just because he doesn't charge a fee. In my experience, a broker who does not charge a fee tends to work with a limited amount of lenders and may very well only recommend lenders that provide the him with the best commission instead of providing the best package for you.

A good mortgage broker will scour the entire marketplace for the best deal to suit your needs. The mortgage broker I use has access to mortgage products that aren't even available to High Street customers!

Currently, buy-to-let mortgages do not fall under the FSA (Financial Services Authority) guidelines. Therefore mortgage brokers can ask for their fee at any time, not just when a mortgage offer is obtained, as is the case with personal mortgages. Many brokers will require their fee on exchange of contracts.

LENDER'S APPLICATION FEE

Almost all lenders charge an application fee. Sometimes this is required as a separate payment; other times the lender will add it to your mortgage. You can expect this fee to cost between £250 and £500.

SURVEYOR'S FEE

Before your mortgage offer is approved you will need to have the property valued by a surveyor. This is so the lender can determine the maximum loan. There is a charge for this service and you should budget for approximately £250.

DEVELOPER 'EXTRAS'

Often, you have the option to customise your property by adding 'optional extras' offered by the developer.

It is worth checking thoroughly with the developer exactly what is fitted as standard in the property, as some of these optional extras are necessary if you plan to rent out or sell the property.

Extras can range widely from kitchen appliance upgrades to an additional shaver point in the en suite. Many developers no longer provide flooring, so it's essential to find out if this is included and budget for it if necessary.

You would be amazed to see the extremes some developers go to in order to make a little more profit. At one housing development I know of even the doors cost extra! At others, items such as doorbells, paving slabs, fencing, lighting and everything else you can possibly imagine are considered an 'extra'. Ridiculous, but true!

The benefit of buying these items from the developer is that:

- You can often add the cost to your mortgage.
- They'll be fitted while the property is being built, thus saving you time.

The downside is most developers charge a premium for extras. In other words, you'll save money by going elsewhere.

Optional extras are usually only available for housing developments rather than new-build flats. In most cases you will be allowed to choose items such as tiling and kitchen units and worktops. However, in some developments these decisions are made by the developer. This helps keep costs down.

STAMP DUTY LAND TAX (SDLT)

You will be required to pay this cost upon completion. The current rates are as follows:

- Up to £120,000 – Zero
- Over £120,000 but not more than £250,000 – 1%
- Over £250,000 but not more than £500,000 – 3%
- Over £500,000 – 4%

In addition, some disadvantaged areas are SDLT exempt. You can check whether an area you are interested in falls under this classification by visiting the Inland Revenue and Customs website at www.hmrc.gov.uk/so/pcode_search.htm

On purchase you must complete an SDLT return and pay the duty within 30 days.

If you're thinking of selling your property immediately on completion you will not be able to avoid SDLT. Back-to-back transactions such as this still require you to complete with the developer and then your purchaser to complete with you. Even if you only own the property for five minutes, you will still have to pay stamp duty as you have technically completed on it. The only way to avoid this is with assignable contracts, where the developer re-issues the contract and removes you from the deal completely.

The Stamp Duty Land Tax rules came into force on 1 December 2003. The rule changes now mean that if you buy more than one property in a single transaction, all the properties are linked and treated as one purchase.

For example, if you bought two properties at £150,000 each, you would reasonably expect to pay 1% stamp duty on each transaction: a total bill of £3,000.

In terms of the new stamp duty rules, however, the transactions are linked, resulting in a total transaction value of £300,000 and a total stamp duty bill of £9,000. Ouch!

PROFESSIONAL SNAGGING INSPECTION FEES

Property inspection companies are discussed in Chapter 11.

Charges vary from company to company but you can expect to pay roughly £300 for a two-bedroom apartment rising to around £500 for a four-bedroom house.

If you are using a property investment company, it may have negotiated a discount for its clients.

FURNISHING YOUR PROPERTY

If you are planning on renting out your property then you need to 'dress it for success'. Gone are the days when you could get away with second-hand furniture from the local junk shop.

Buying cheap or second-hand furniture is a false economy anyway. If it is cheap it won't last long and if it's second-hand and worn, it will take you a lot longer to attract tenants.

I would advise investors to employ the services of a professional furnishing company that deals strictly with investment properties. A good company will provide you with everything you need from cutlery to flooring, sofas and curtains.

This is an ideal service if you do not live in close proximity to the property or you are too busy to arrange it all.

Dealing through furniture companies can cost you a lot less than buying directly from High Street stores.

On average you can expect to pay between £2,500 and £4,500 to fully furnish a one-bedroom apartment and £5,000 or more for a two-bedroom apartment.

It is important to discuss your target market with your letting agent. Some agents will tell you that items such as DVD players, stereos and TVs are all expected as part of the rental package. If you offer less than the competition your property will take longer to rent out. Property in some areas may not need furnishing at all and the rental income difference between furnished and unfurnished may be negligible.

If you want to sell your property to realise the capital growth, then you can very often hire a furniture package from the same companies.

If the property doesn't have flooring, you could consider offering to pay for this as part of an incentive package for prospective buyers. Even if you increase the price of the property to take account of the extra cost, it should be a good selling point.

Chapter 11

Snagging

We had just moved into our brand new house and, that evening, I decided to take a bath. Afterwards I noticed a growing pool of water on the floor under the tub. It turned out that the plumber, or perhaps his young 'apprentice', had forgotten to attach the drainage pipe. Luckily, the panel was off and I noticed it straight away, otherwise I would have soon found the tub in the kitchen below!

Interestingly, on further inspection, drainage pipes hadn't been connected in two showers, the other bathtub or the kitchen sink! Needless to say, I was not impressed.

Snagging is one of the most important aspects of buying property off-plan – so important that I have decided to devote a whole chapter to it.

If you have never experienced buying a new-build property to live in or as an investment, then you could be in for some surprises.

These days, many developers do not employ their own bricklayers, joiners, plumbers, electricians and other tradesmen: all these jobs are subcontracted. In fact one building site manager recently told me that over 100 tradesmen were used to build each house. As you can imagine, this creates serious quality control problems.

Developers often struggle to find good quality tradesmen who take pride in their work.

Unfortunately, many people are under the illusion that a brand new house or apartment is going to be picture perfect – like when you buy a new car! Sadly, this is often very far from the truth.

In many cases when people purchase an investment property, particularly from plan, they live nowhere near their property. In fact, probably at least three quarters of our clients will never actually set foot in their properties. A lot of people either assume that there won't be any snagging issues or expect that their estate or letting agent will deal with the snagging for them.

Whether investors are planning to rent out or sell their properties, prospective tenants or buyers are going to be immediately turned off if they see any evidence of outstanding snagging issues.

Obviously, you will either want to rent out or sell your property as quickly as possible. The last thing you want is the property to lie vacant for many months because of issues that could have been dealt with promptly from the start.

According to professional snagging company Inspector Home:

"New Homes are exempt from the Sale of Goods Act 1994 – if you purchase a home that is faulty, you cannot take it back, you cannot get a refund, and you have to allow your builder a 'reasonable' amount of time to put it right for you before you can take them to court. You have no legal right to compensation for the stress and inconvenience of living in an unfinished home, and if you try to pull out of the sale your builder will probably sue you – successfully."

I hope that after reading this you realise the importance of having your property professionally snagged.

Case Study

One of our clients was being pushed to complete on a property but refused to settle because there were so many outstanding issues.

For just £300 a well-known snagging company was commissioned to inspect the apartment. The report, along with pictures, was sent to our client's solicitor, the developer's solicitor and the developer.

The report showed that the apartment was suffering from quite serious structural defects, and many other issues, and as a result the developer and his solicitor backed down and agreed to attend to the issues before completion.

Because the snagging report came from a highly respected third-party snagging inspection company, our client had more clout and was listened to by the developer.

Another reason why it is important to use a professional snagging company is because it will identify issues that people like you and I are totally unaware of.

When we purchased our most recent property we popped in before the snagging company did its inspection and counted around 50 problems that needed fixing. After the snagging company finished its inspection they had found 200 problems!

Chapter 12

Back-to-back and Assignable Contract Transactions

'Back-to-back', and 'assignable contracts' are how investors 'flip' or 'turn' their properties. These are the terms used to describe selling the property on to another buyer on completion and (hopefully) making a profit in the process. It's an exciting way to make money when the property market is buoyant.

Back-to-back transactions are when you complete on a property but a new buyer completes almost simultaneously. It will be the new buyer's funds that pay the developer and any funds left over will be your profit. Your new buyer may have exchanged contracts with you some time before this transaction completes.

Many people confuse back-to-back with assignable contracts. The main difference is that, with assignable contracts, the developer agrees to re-assign the contracts to the new buyer. However, should the new buyer fail to complete, it is more than likely that you will be responsible for the purchase and the debt owed to the developer.

When the property market is booming and there is huge demand for property, flipping can be an easy way of making money. However, a word or two of warning is required:

- With the end of the buy-to-let boom opportunities to sell property back-to-back or with assignable contracts are becoming much more rare. These types of deals usually only work when there is a strong demand from investors and end-users wanting to buy property.

- You will not see the money in your bank account until after legal completion of the property with the new buyer. Selling 'before' completion doesn't actually happen in practice.

- Completion dates on new-builds can vary enormously. The developer may end up months ahead of schedule or months behind schedule. If you, or the person buying the property from you, are not prepared for this eventuality, then you may both find yourselves in financial difficulty.

- If you cannot find a new buyer before completion or, as often happens, the buyer you had lined up backs out, you will be obliged to complete on the property. If you do not have a mortgage offer in place to cover you in these circumstances, then you may find yourself in serious financial difficulty.

  Make sure you get in touch with a mortgage adviser at least three months prior to completion in order to have your offer ready in time.

HOW BACK-TO-BACK WORKS

Here's an example of how a typical back-to-back transaction might work:

- You reserve a property that is not due for completion for 18 months. The property has a list price of £100,000.

- Shortly after reserving you exchange contracts at a price of £95,000, giving you a discount of 5%.

- Approximately five to six months before completion you instruct an estate agent to market the property. Of course, the price has to be more than £95,000 for you to make a profit.

- You find a buyer who is prepared to pay £115,000 and exchange contracts with you.

- On the day of completion the following takes place:

    - The new buyer's solicitor transfers the purchase price (£115,000) into your solicitor's account.
    - Your solicitor transfers your purchase price (£95,000) to the developer's solicitor.
    - Your solicitor transfers the balance (£20,000 minus costs) into your bank account.

The profit of £20,000 is 'gross' and excludes legal fees and other costs.

HOW TO CARRY OUT A BACK-TO-BACK SALE

Make sure your contract with the developer allows you to sell and there are no clauses that restrict your ability to market and sell the property.

Typical clauses may include:

- Not being allowed to market the property until the show house or show flat has been sold.

- Strict clauses regarding when the contracts can be sold on (a year after they were signed by the initial buyer, for example).

- Not being allowed to use the developer's sales agents or marketing material.

- Not being allowed to advertise the property, including signage, until after a certain time.

Some clauses I have seen have been restrictive in the extreme, such as:

- Not being able to market the property in the same geographical area as the development.
- Not being able to use a set list of estate agents in the area.
- Not being able to use images or floor plans of the property that are deemed to be the developer's intellectual property.
- Only being able to sell after receiving confirmation from the developer and using their sales agents.
- Not being allowed to advertise the property until after the developer has sold all of its properties and is off site.

The developer's view in all of this is that they don't want to create competition for the properties they still have to sell. With regard to the floor plans, pictures and all of the developer's marketing material, the developer is well within its right to withhold this information from you.

ASSIGNABLE CONTRACTS

Assignable contracts are similar to back-to-back in theory. They enable the investor to sell on the contract for the property after exchange of contracts but before legal completion. Although it is a reasonably 'normal' transaction, not all developers allow this. If you are relying on making your money this way you should check what the developer will and will not allow before exchanging contracts. The obvious benefit to the investor here is that any capital growth in the property can be enjoyed without having to raise a mortgage or pay stamp duty.

SOME KEY POINTS ABOUT BACK-TO-BACK AND ASSIGNABLE CONTRACTS

- If you are buying in a development where you know that there are a number of other investors who also wish to flip their properties, then it makes sense to band together to market your properties collectively, perhaps through an estate agency. Not only will you be able to negotiate better rates for the advertising but you will also be able to gain consensus on the pricing level, enhancing everyone's likelihood of a sale.

- The property is not sold until it's sold. Make sure you have a mortgage in case your new buyer pulls out at the last minute and you have to complete on the property. Bear in mind that the mortgage offer process can take up to several months... months in which you could suffer severe financial penalties if you or your new buyer are unable to complete.

- Developers like you to think that if an off-plan investment property is sold on to a new buyer then they are no longer responsible for any snagging issues. Not so! Developers are responsible for any defects in their building for a period of up to two years after construction. This applies to the property, not the owner.

  This is ultimately dependent, however, on what type of guarantee the developer is providing (for example, a Zurich Building Guarantee or an NHBC Warranty or even an Architect's Certificate). Your solicitor should be able to provide you with this information and any professional snagging company will know who is responsible for what – so call them and pick their brains!

  If you are selling back-to-back or assigning the contracts you may not be able or willing to carry out the pre-completion inspection. You then have a couple of options open to you:

- Tell your new buyer, via the estate agent or solicitor, that they are covered by the builder's guarantee and should not be put off by the developer's denials. I have lived in new developments where buyers of investors' properties (not mine) have suffered a silent hell of flooding, shoddy workmanship and plumbing disasters. At every point the developer denied responsibility, when in fact it was theirs. And all of these new owners were first-time buyers with young families. The developer immediately changed his tune once a professional snagging company became involved!

- Invite your buyer to the pre-completion snagging. Even though you are planning to sell back-to-back, you are still entitled to this check, and as you're not going to live there, why not allow the person who is to snag it? This way they have complete control over what remedial work needs to be done. If you can't make the inspection – perhaps it's too far to travel – let the developer know that someone will be attending in your place.

- In all cases, let your buyer know about the professional inspection companies that are available to them to help resolve any problems they might encounter.

- Of course, if you haven't been able to re-sell your property prior to completion, then you will need to deal with snagging – whether on your own or through a snagging company. It is important that any problems such as poor workmanship and items that are not working are corrected, so that potential new buyers see nothing but a clean palette, instead of problems and bad paint jobs.

Chapter 13

Investing Abroad

Over the last ten years the lure of making big profits has attracted many British property investors abroad. Spain has traditionally been the most popular destination but there has also been a huge amount of interest in recent years in the 'accession' countries – those that have just joined the EU. These include Cyprus, the Czech Republic, Estonia, Hungary, Latvia, Lithuania, Malta, Poland, Slovakia and Slovenia.

Prague in the Czech Republic is a good example of the interest in the emerging markets of Europe. Tipped to be the 'Dublin of the East', prices have soared by as much as 100% in many areas over the last two to three years.

Traditional American investment destinations such as Florida are still proving attractive to British investors, while new investment markets, such as Panama, are starting to open up.

Buying off-plan property overseas offers you the same benefits as buying UK off-plan property:

- You can buy property at a discount.
- Your property can rise in value during the construction phase.
- You can easily compare the price to similar properties in the area.
- You can benefit from phased price increases.
- You can sell your property and realise the growth, or keep it to rent out.

Investing overseas also offers a number of additional benefits:

- **Higher yields.** Rental yields of 10% or more are not uncommon in many countries, especially emerging market countries. The higher the rental yield the easier it is to pay your mortgage and other expenses or earn an attractive income from your investment.

- **Cheaper properties.** It's possible to buy properties in some countries for as little as £30,000.

- **Holiday accommodation.** If you buy in a country you love you can use the property for holidays or, ultimately, as a retirement home.

Against this you should remember that a high rental yield in a foreign country is not attractive if mortgage interest rates in that country are much higher than in the UK. And just because a property is cheap doesn't make it a good deal.

Buying property overseas also exposes you to a myriad of additional risks and problems, especially if you invest in emerging markets:

- **Property sourcing.** Unless you know the country intimately how do you know which is the best part of Warsaw, Budapest or Riga to invest in?

- **Legal protection.** Some countries do not offer the same legal infrastructure and protection of property rights that we take for granted in Britain. In other words, you are more likely to get ripped off!

- **Currency risk.** Property prices may be rising in your chosen country but if the local currency is falling in value at the same time you may actually be losing money overall. Of course, if the local currency is rising in value against the pound this will provide a boost to your profits.

- **Language barrier.** This can make it difficult to conduct negotiations and review important legal documents.

- **Taxes.** You may have to pay all sorts of taxes and other charges. However, many of these can be offset against your UK tax liability.

- **Funding.** You will probably have to come up with a much larger deposit than you would in the UK. It is not uncommon to pay a deposit of between 20% and 40%. This places much more of your money at risk should something go wrong.

Many of the above problems can be overcome by using one of the many English-speaking property investment companies that will source property for you and help you through the buying process. They will also introduce you to solicitors, letting agents and mortgage providers.

If you know very little about the country in which you're investing, you are totally dependent on the property company that is advising you. Unless you have complete confidence in their investment skills and integrity you are taking a very big risk.

How do you find a firm that is good at picking profitable properties and which you can trust? There's no easy answer, unfortunately. Word of mouth is usually the best way but don't expect to find many old established property investment companies out there – most having only been going for a few years.

DOING YOUR RESEARCH

As with UK property, researching your chosen overseas investment location and the company selling the development is extremely important. Unless you are a seasoned visitor to your chosen destination, you may find this quite difficult. However, you should always persevere to avoid making a costly mistake.

From the very outset, make sure you understand all of the costs of making a property purchase from start to finish. That means all legal costs, all taxes (national and local) and especially all 'hidden' costs.

Other important things you should find out include:

- **The size of the development.** There are many developments that have or will have hundreds of properties. Having a property that is part of an extensive building site could create problems when you start trying to rent it out, especially if there are lots of other investors trying to do the same thing. Some larger sites may take many years to complete. It is important that you understand the developer's plans and how this might affect your use of the property. Happy holidaymakers won't be happy for long if they're woken at seven every morning by noisy construction workers.

- **The state of the letting market.** If you're buying to rent out to tourists, research things such as travel time to the closest airport, how easy it is to access shops, beaches, golf courses, restaurants and points of interest. Find out when during the year it will be busy and when it will be quiet. Will the anticipated rental income during the high season cover the mortgage during the low season? Find out also whether the agent dealing with your purchase will also handle the rental for you.

- **Research the developer and sales agent.** Ask to see other developments they have built and speak to the people living there. Visit online forums and ask if anybody else has had any experience of the developer. It is a sad truth that the overseas property market is awash with crooks waiting to part the gullible investor from his money. It is sometimes difficult to separate the respectable from the dishonest, particularly if you do not know what is expected from the developer and the 'correct' way of buying a property in that country and the best way to protect your funds.

Case Study

One of my clients, a solicitor, fell victim to a dishonest property developer. He and his friends clubbed together to buy a beautiful apartment in Spain. They were provided with fancy brochures, layouts, specifications and even a free trip to meet with the developer, visit the site and select their fixtures and fittings. They had no idea what was in store for them.

They paid their reservation fee and their 30% deposit, which in this case was close to £80,000. Being a solicitor, he decided that he would deal with the legal aspects and save them a bit of money.

After the deposits were paid, they were in touch with the developer a few times more. It was a long build programme and they were told that everything was progressing and was on schedule.

Finally the day came when they made a phone call to book a viewing appointment, as one of the purchasers was going to be in the area. Imagine their concern when the phone call didn't go through.... ever again.

The friends rushed out to Spain to see what was going on and saw exactly what they had seen months before – untouched land.

It turned out that the developer never actually owned the land to begin with. It had made up nice, glossy brochures and had the whole thing worked out perfectly, including legal contracts. Now this company is at least £80,000 richer and, because the purchasers never confirmed that their deposits were being paid in to an escrow account (held by a neutral third party), everybody involved lost a lot money.

The most concerning part is that obviously our clients were not the only buyers in this 'development' – they were just one of many who were taken for a very expensive ride.

KNOW THE LAW

It's very important that you have a basic understanding of the laws surrounding purchasing property within your chosen country. At the very least this will prepare you for any little surprises that crop up during the transaction. In some countries, for example, foreign nationals are not allowed to own property. Instead, you must set up a company within that country and have the company purchase the property.

In many cases, the overseas developer will put you in touch with a solicitor who can speak English. Although this can be very helpful, it is important to make sure that you trust the developer and the solicitor they are recommending.

If possible, it is advisable to hire your own solicitor. If you do not know anybody who can recommend one, then ask the British Embassy or Consul in that country. They may be able to provide you with an approved list of lawyers in your area who can speak English, although they won't be able to recommend any. Once you have chosen your lawyer, advise him that you will need your contracts and any other supporting documentation translated into English.

Before you sign anything, make sure it is reviewed by your solicitor and that you are aware of all the local practices relating to property purchases. Every country is different.

In Spain, for example, it is important that you see what is called the Escritura Publica, which contains all the relevant details, description and location of the property. It is also a record of any debts against the property, such as a mortgage.

Foreign investors have recently been snapping up newly built property in Northern Cyprus, even though the ownership of much of the land is hotly disputed. Greek Cypriots forced to flee to the south in 1974 say the land is still theirs.

The contract price is also very important. Find out if the price is expressed in the local currency such as Euros or in Pounds Sterling (some UK companies who have a company in other countries will charge in Sterling). If the price is expressed in Euros, for example, you could be in for an expensive surprise if there has been a significant change in the exchange rate and the pound is worth less than when you did your original calculations.

You also need to know if there are going to be taxes added to the purchase price. For example, in Spain you will need to add an extra 7% 'IVA' which is the Spanish equivalent of VAT.

TIP

When purchasing your off-plan property, make sure that the contract makes provision for your payments (deposit etc.) to go into an escrow account, to which the developer has no access until completion. This will protect your money should anything go wrong with the development. Most reputable developers will offer this. If they don't and something does go wrong, you will have a lengthy and potentially unsuccessful battle to get your money back.

FINANCING YOUR PROPERTY

Overseas off-plan property purchases can work very differently to those in the UK. You will sometimes be required to make staged payments and these payments can be quite large. It is not unusual for a developer to expect a 30-40% deposit from the buyer within a month or two of reserving the property, with the balance paid in three instalments over the course of the build, typically 20-30%.

Your initial reservation costs may also be quite large. Whereas in the UK, reservation fees can start from as little as £500, I have seen a going rate of £10,000 for some overseas off-plan reservations. It's worth noting that your reservation fee will probably be non-refundable, so it is very important that you are absolutely certain you want to invest.

The existence of mortgage products and your ability to qualify for one will vary from country to country. Spain, for example, has a mature foreign national investor market and obtaining a mortgage there would be easier than in one of the Eastern European countries.

Although mortgage products may be available in your chosen country, they will be different to UK mortgages and UK buy-to-let mortgages in particular. For example, the amount of deposit required will be different.

The developer may have put together a package of lenders for you to use but it is always advisable to consult with your chosen solicitor or broker before signing anything.

The advantage of using a local source of finance is that you can protect yourself from currency risk. If your mortgage payments are expressed in Sterling but your rental income is expressed in the local currency any sharp move in the exchange rate could leave you with a serious shortfall.

There are now many UK-based English-speaking firms specialising in arranging overseas mortgages, which can be easily found by a quick search on the internet.

The benefit of using such a firm is that it will be easily accessible and will have to comply with certain standards. The downside is that it may cost you more.

THE INTRODUCTION TRIP

Many developers will offer a reasonably priced trip to the country to introduce you to the development. The trip will normally last for between two and four days and the cost will generally include flights, transport and accommodation. Often, should you decide to purchase one of their properties, they will deduct the cost of your trip from the price of the property.

Make no mistake, though. You are not going on a holiday: you will be attending a sales presentation. Although many of the companies who run such trips claim that they don't use high-pressure sales tactics, this is their business, and their business is to sell you a property before you hop on the plane back to the UK.

Some companies may request that you bring a banker's draft with you. This is understandable, of course, as the developer wants to sell property; they are not interested in offering cheap getaways to people who are neither interested in their development or do not have the financial resources to purchase a property.

It is very important not to get caught up in all of the hype. Let's face it, gorgeous weather, sunny beaches, lovely food and cheap wine, not to mention perhaps very reasonably priced properties can all be very tempting. Do not leave your head at the airport. It is always important to do your own due diligence on the development, the developer and the area. Be prepared to say 'no'.

HIDDEN COSTS

When buying property overseas, there will be many other costs and fees associated with the purchase that you are most likely unfamiliar with if you have only purchased property in the UK. It is vital that you know *exactly* what all of the costs involved in the purchase are *and* what the maintenance and management of the property will cost (for example, letting agents, cleaning, service charges and so on).

If you took advantage of a developer's introduction trip, then you can be sure that the sparkling new show-home you were taken to was fitted out with the best possible fixtures and fittings. Find out exactly what is included in the price and what is not. Items that a UK investor will normally take for granted as part of the package may not be included when purchasing abroad:

- White goods
- Heating

- Air-conditioning
- Flooring
- Water heater
- Landscaping (including pool)

You may not think that central heating is important while visiting in lovely warm temperatures. However, during the colder season it will certainly play a role in the comfort of your holiday-let tenants, not to mention you.

On top of the extra costs for fittings and fixtures, there may also be unexpected local or national taxes to pay. For instance, did you know:

- There is a 10% tax due on completion in Italy.
- You should add 7% tax to the purchase cost in Spain.
- A local community tax is payable by all property owners, whether resident or non-resident, in Italy.
- Taxe foncière is a land tax and is paid by the owner of the property in France.
- The owner of a property in Dubai must visit every six months to continue to qualify for residency.

If you are accustomed to paying just 1-3% stamp duty in the UK, then some of these unexpected costs could come as a bit of a surprise. Of course, the hope is that you have researched your investment area soundly and have budgeted for all of these extra costs.

Selling your property can also expose you to extra costs. Depending on which country your property is in, you could be subject to local capital gains tax. Estate agent fees may also be much higher than in the UK. In Spain, for example, you can expect to pay between 5% and 10%.

If you are successfully renting your property then you may also be liable for income tax in the country your property is located. Non-resident owners of Spanish property have to pay 25% income tax on 2% of the official rated value of the property.

Other costs that you will most likely be responsible for are ones similar to service charges in the UK that cover such things as communal maintenance of pools and gardens. If you are buying a villa in a big development you may also need to pay fees for lighting, roads and other communal areas.

COMPLETION DATES

As with UK off-plan properties, overseas developments can take anywhere from 9 to 24 months to complete and you should only take the developer's time-scale as a guideline.

CASE STUDY

I have clients who live in Spain and, due to their work, are re-located every four to five years. Before this couple moved to Spain, they commenced the purchasing process of an off-plan villa in what they considered to be an exceptional location. The developer told them that completion would take place in one year. Therefore, they decided to rent an apartment during the construction phase and have at least three or four years in their nice new home.

Unfortunately, the 12-month build programme has now taken over four years! The property is being built, albeit slowly, however, this unfortunate couple have now been posted somewhere else and will be unable to enjoy their property!

Although four years is just plain crazy and probably very unusual, it is important to remember that builders' completion dates are merely guidelines. Certainly don't make plans based around these dates!

Equally make sure that you do have enough funds available in case they complete on time – the one time that you count on the builder's being behind schedule, you can almost guarantee that they will be on track!

Conclusion

I sincerely hope that you have found the information in this book useful.

As you have read, there can be a whole host of pitfalls and issues to be aware of when buying property from plan. However, there are also some fantastic positive aspects. Provided that you invest from a knowledgeable and informed background, you should be in a position to minimise your risks and maximise your profits.

As with all investment, there is an element of risk involved. However, in property investment, although there are certain aspects that are simply out of your control, there are also many other aspects that you can control by investing knowledgeably.

Hopefully this book has provided you with a good basis on what is vital to understand about investing in off-plan property, including mortgages, what to look for in good investment property and what to be aware of should you choose to work with a property investment company.

The most important thing is that you are empowered by understanding the key points and issues. Armed with this information you will hopefully be able to make informed decisions and invest wisely.

Happy, and safe, investing!
Alyssa Savage
David Savage

Glossary of Terms

It is important that you have an understanding of the terms and concepts that are used throughout this book. Please take a moment to read through this section and feel free to refer back to it as and when you need to.

Assignable Contracts – This is where you sell the property on by exchanging contracts with a new buyer after you have exchanged contracts with the developer. This transaction occurs before legal completion. It will be the new buyer's funds that pay the developer for the purchase price you originally agreed and exchanged contracts on, with any remaining difference in funds as your gross profit. Not all developers allow this so check with them before committing yourself. Even though you may have assigned the contracts to a new buyer, you are still most likely to be liable for the debt if the new buyer does not complete.

Back-To-Back – This is where you complete on a property and a new buyer that you have found completes with you almost simultaneously. It will be the new buyer's funds that pay the developer and any funds left over will be your profit.

Conclusion of Missives - This is the terminology used in Scotland for a similar process to Exchange of Contracts. It is the stage at which the contract (missives) to purchase becomes binding on both parties. In Scotland, Conclusion of Missives occurs generally within 14 days of reservation. For ease of reference in this book, the term 'Exchange of Contracts' should also be taken to mean 'Conclusion of Missives'.

Completion – Final stage in legally transferring ownership of a property when the contract of sale is completed. The vendor hands over the property and the buyer pays the purchase price. It is at this point that the mortgage starts. It is when the funds go from your solicitor's account and into the vendor's solicitor's account.

Deposit – Many people get confused about the deposits required when purchasing off-plan property. There are generally two required:

- **First Deposit:** The developer requires the first deposit on Exchange of Contracts. In most cases this will be between 5% and 10% of the purchase price. This amount will count towards the final deposit required by your mortgage provider.

- **Second Deposit:** Most lenders require a minimum deposit of 15% on buy-to-let mortgages. You will be required to provide these funds to your solicitor prior to completion. This deposit plus your mortgage (minus the deposit paid to the lender) will make up the outstanding balance to be transferred to the developer's solicitor on completion.

DiP – Decision in Principle - An indication of the likely outcome of a mortgage application. This is not a formal offer but includes a credit check with a credit reference agency and an assessment of your ability to repay the loan amount requested. Some DiPs can last up to six months, while others can last only 30 days. A DiP is useful to highlight any credit problems you might have but were previously unaware of.

Discount – Many property investment companies negotiate discounts with developers and pass these on to their property investor clients. Discounts typically range from 5% to 25%. Discounts are a controversial area of off-plan property investment. Many have been found to be artificially created: developers simply raise their list prices and then reduce them when asked for a discount.

However, some discounts are worth snapping up and some property investment companies do use their bulk-buying power to acquire property for their clients for less than the true market value.

Exchange of Contracts – This is the first major deadline when buying property off-plan. In England and Wales, Exchange of Contracts usually occurs 28 days after the property has been reserved.

At this stage a deposit of 5% to 10% is paid to the developer.

When you and the developer exchange contracts the deal becomes legally binding. If you pull out before completion you will lose your deposit and may find yourself being sued by the developer.

The contract will state the price, what fixtures and fittings are included in the deal, and the date when completion will take place.

You should also have a mortgage offer in place at this point. Some solicitors will not go to Exchange of Contracts without one.

Gearing – Borrowing to buy property, using the rental income to cover the mortgage payments. If property prices rise, gearing magnifies your capital profits because you get to enjoy growth on a much larger chunk of property than you could normally afford. And if property prices fall, gearing magnifies your losses.

Gifted deposit – Where the builder gifts you up to usually 5% of the purchase price. Some lenders will accept a gifted deposit in lieu of a deposit paid by the property purchaser, others will not.

Handover – When the funds for the purchase pass from your solicitor to the vendor's solicitor. It is at this point that keys to the property are handed over to you.

Reservation and Reservation Fees – The initial fee required by the developer to hold a property for you, generally £500 to £1,000. This fee may or may not be fully or partially refundable so make sure you read the reservation papers. If you are not prepared to proceed to Exchange of Contracts, you may very well have to forfeit your reservation fee.

Rental Cover – Lenders usually insist that the monthly rental income from a property should equal at least 125% of the mortgage payments. This can go up to 130% and beyond and will vary from lender to lender and between buy-to-let mortgage products.

Shortfall – This is the difference between what you would expect to pay as a deposit for a buy-to-let mortgage (based on the lender's rental coverage criteria) and what you can actually raise as a mortgage based upon the current level of interest rates and the projected rental income for your property.

Snagging – When your property is finally built the developer will ask you to take a walk around your unit in order to find any outstanding issues that need fixing. Don't ever think that because you are buying a new property it is going to be in perfect condition. I highly recommend that you use a professional snagging company.

Pay Less Tax!

... with help from Taxcafe's unique tax guides and software

All products available online at www.taxcafe.co.uk

- **How to Avoid Property Tax.** Essential reading for property investors who want to know all the tips and tricks to follow to pay less tax on their property profits.

- **Using a Property Company to Save Tax.** How to massively increase your profits by using a property company... plus all the traps to avoid.

- **Retire Rich with a Property Pension.** How to buy property at a 40% discount and completely avoid income tax and capital gains tax by using a personal pension plan.

- **How to Avoid Inheritance Tax.** A-Z of inheritance tax planning, with clear explanations & numerous examples. Covers simple & sophisticated tax planning.

- **How to Avoid Stamp Duty.** Little-known trade secrets that will help you reduce or eliminate the stamp duty bill when you buy property.

- **Non Resident & Offshore Tax Planning.** How to exploit non resident tax status to reduce your tax bill, plus advice on using offshore trusts and companies.

- **How to Avoid Tax on Your Stock Market Profits.** This guide contains detailed advice on how to pay less capital gains tax, income tax and inheritance tax on your stock market investments and dealings.

- **Using a Company to Save Tax.** Everything you need to know about the tax benefits of using a company to run your business.

- **Bonus vs Dividend.** Shows how shareholder/directors of companies can save thousands in tax by choosing the optimal mix of bonus and dividends.

- **Selling a Sole Trader Business.** A potential minefield with numerous traps to avoid but significant tax saving opportunities.

- **How to Claim Tax Credits.** Even families with higher incomes can make successful tax credit claims. This guide shows how much you can claim and how to go about it.

- **Property Capital Gains Tax Calculator.** Unique software that performs complex capital gains tax calculations in seconds.

Disclaimer

Please note that this guide is intended as general guidance only for individual readers and does NOT constitute investment or other professional advice. Taxcafe UK Limited accepts no responsibility or liability for loss which may arise from reliance on information contained in this guide.

We therefore recommend that for investment or other professional advice you consult a suitably qualified professional adviser. Please also note that your personal circumstances may vary from the general examples given in this guide and your professional adviser will be able to give specific advice based on your personal circumstances.

Printed in the United Kingdom
by Lightning Source UK Ltd.
119585UK00001B/100-111

9 781904 608301